DEREK INTRODUCES
THE CONSTITUTION AND PARLIAMENT OF INDIA

Derek O'Brien was born in Kolkata. He began his career as a journalist for *Sportsworld* magazine but soon shifted to advertising. After working for a number of very successful years as Creative Head of Ogilvy, Derek decided to focus all his energy and talent in his passion—quizzing.

Today, Derek is Asia's best-known quizmaster and the CEO of Derek O'Brien & Associates. He is the host of the longest-running game show on Indian television, the *Cadbury Bournvita Quiz Contest*, for which he was voted the Best Anchor of a Game Show at the Indian Television Academy Awards for three years in a row. Always innovating, Derek is also credited with having conducted the first quiz on Twitter in 2010.

Derek has written over fifty bestselling reference, quiz and textbooks. In 2011, he was voted to the Rajya Sabha as a member of Parliament (MP) and is the Leader of the Trinamool Congress in the Rajya Sabha.

Keep in touch with Derek on Twitter, where his handle is @quizderek.

Other books by Derek O'Brien
(from Rupa Publications)

Bournvita Quiz Contest Quiz Book 2012

*The Ultimate Bournvita Quiz Contest Book of Knowledge
(Volumes 1 and 2)*

The Best of Bournvita Quiz Contest

*Speak Up, Speak Out: My Favourite Elocution Pieces and
How to Deliver Them*

My Way: Success Mantras of 12 Achievers

Derek Introduces 100 Iconic Indians

DEREK INTRODUCES
THE CONSTITUTION AND PARLIAMENT OF INDIA

Derek O'Brien

Published in Red Turtle by
Rupa Publications India Pvt. Ltd 2015
7/16, Ansari Road, Daryaganj
New Delhi 110002

Sales Centres:

Allahabad Bengaluru Chennai
Hyderabad Jaipur Kathmandu
Kolkata Mumbai

Copyright © Derek O'Brien & Associates 2015

All rights reserved.
No part of this publication may be reproduced, transmitted, or stored in a
retrieval system, in any form or by any means, electronic,
mechanical, photocopying, recording or otherwise,
without the prior permission of the publisher.

ISBN: 978-81-291-3655-8

Second impression 2016

10 9 8 7 6 5 4 3 2

Moral right of the author has been asserted.

Printed at Thomson Press India Ltd., Faridabad

This book is sold subject to the condition that it shall not,
by way of trade or otherwise, be lent, resold, hired out, or otherwise
circulated, without the publisher's prior consent, in any form of binding or
cover other than that in which it is published.

CONTENTS

Introduction ix

SECTION A: THE CONSTITUTION OF INDIA

The Making of the Constitution—The Constituent Assembly 2

The Making of the Constitution—Select People Involved 6
- B. R. Ambedkar 6
- Jawaharlal Nehru 8
- Maulana Abul Kalam Azad 10
- Rajendra Prasad 11
- Sardar Vallabhbhai Patel 13
- Sarojini Naidu 15
- Vijaya Lakshmi Pandit 16
- Other Leaders 18

The Constitution—Its Features, Structure and Provisions 22
- The Book and Its Salient Features 22
- Structure of the Constitution of India: Articles, Parts and Schedules 25
- Preamble to the Constitution 27
- The Union and Its Territory 29
- Citizenship 31
- Fundamental Rights and Fundamental Duties 33
- Directive Principles of State Policy 36
- The Union Executive: The President of India 37

Short Biographies of Presidents of India	40
The Union Executive: The Vice President of India	48
The Union Legislature: Parliament of India	49
The State Executive: The Governor	49
The State Legislature	51
Council of Ministers and the Chief Minister	55
Judiciary	56
Union Territories	61
Panchayats	61
Municipalities	63
Relations between the Union and the States	65
Finance	66
Services under the Union and the States	68
Elections	69
Special Classes	70
Official Language of India	72
Emergency Provisions	74
Amendments to the Constitution of India	75

SECTION B: THE PARLIAMENT OF INDIA

The Parliament House	81
The Lok Sabha	83
History, Composition and Term	83
Presiding Officers of the Lok Sabha: The Speaker and the Deputy Speaker	86
The Leader of the House and the Leader of the Opposition in the Lok Sabha	88
Council of Ministers	89
The Prime Minister of India	90
Short Biographies of Prime Ministers of India	91
General Elections	100

The Rajya Sabha	110
History, Composition and Term	110
Presiding Officers of the Rajya Sabha: The Chairman and the Deputy Chairman	113
The Leader of the House and the Leader of the Opposition in the Rajya Sabha	113
Union Budget and Bills	117
Union Budget	117
Bills	118
Appendix 1: Outstanding Parliamentarians	125
Appendix 2: Some Famous Speeches Associated with the Parliament of India	135
Appendix 3: Table of Precedence	140
Appendix 4: Election Symbols (as of 2014)	144
Appendix 5: Union, State and Concurrent Lists	156
Bibliography	173

INTRODUCTION

Twenty-seven years as a quizmaster. Twelve years in politics. People often ask me how the journey from quizmaster to parliamentarian has been. I have learned so much as a quizmaster—both on stage and in front of the camera—and in Parliament, the biggest stage of them all, the hallowed portals of Parliament House. As a parliamentarian, each day is a challenge. The one companion, the one resource, the one document I always refer to for my work there, is the Constitution of India.

HOW DID WE GET OUR CONSTITUTION?

With more than 120-crore people, India is the second largest country in the world in terms of population. It is widely regarded as the largest democracy where the ultimate power rests with its citizens. In 1947, after we gained independence from the British and their authoritarian rule, we became a democratic country where every citizen was equal, and could participate in the electoral process.

The idea of democracy was taken further, when our leaders opted for the parliamentary system of government after considering the merits and demerits of other systems. They felt that the presidential system of government (like in the USA) gave more stability but less responsibility by vesting great powers in the President.

A study of the British parliamentary system of government yielded better results. It gave more responsibility to the elected leaders, but there was less stability as this system of government was dependent upon a majority in Parliament and the assessment of responsibility of the Executive was done both on a daily and a periodic basis. While the daily monitoring was carried out by the members of Parliament, through debates, resolutions, no-confidence motions, adjournment motions and other methods, the periodic assessment was done by the citizens at the time of elections, usually held every five years.

Our leaders, after careful consideration, chose responsibility over stability. They believed that a vast country like India, with its great diversity and complexity, needed a system that allowed its people to voice their problems and be heard. The parliamentary system provided this opportunity more than other systems.

Another reason for adopting this system, as pointed out by Mahatma Gandhi, was that the roots of this system were embedded in our heritage through institutions that had been in existence for ages like the village panchayats. Dr. B. R. Ambedkar too stated that Buddhist *sanghas* existing in ancient India were essentially parliamentary type of institutions.

To trace the evolution of the Constitution of India, we need to go back in time by a few centuries. India is an ancient land, ruled by kings who were born here as well as those who came from various parts of the world. After the Mughals, parts of it were under the control of different rulers at various points of time including the British, Portuguese, French, Dutch and Danish, all of whom came to India first as traders and then began to control and exploit the resources. After the First War of Indian Independence in 1857 (or the Revolt of 1857), the British managed to take direct control of the administration in India through the Government of India Act, 1858. By this Act, power was transferred from the British East India Company to the British Crown. This Act provided no room for the participation of the people of India in the decision-making process. In the years that followed, there was a gradual relaxation of control through various reform measures including the Government of India Act, 1935. This Act served as the basis of the future Constitution of India.

Why did the British begin to give more powers to their subjects? There were a number of reasons. For one, they found that they needed to connect with the masses in order to govern. The people therefore needed to have a greater say in the affairs of their own country. The other reason was the rising demand for Indian independence. They had to appease the leaders of the freedom struggle whose demand for independence became more forceful—from dominion status to complete independence. A few months before independence, the Constituent Assembly was established and entrusted with the responsibility of drawing up the Constitution of independent India.

WHY DO WE NEED A CONSTITUTION?

The Constitution of India lays down the rules, principles and ideas on which India is governed. It puts forth the basic framework of various institutions like the Parliament, the Supreme Court of India and the Election Commission of India. It outlines the powers and duties of key posts like the President of India and the Vice President of India. It provides the framework and defines and assigns different responsibilities to the three organs of the state: Legislature, Executive and Judiciary. (While the Legislature makes laws for the nation, the Executive puts them into operation and the Judiciary safeguards them.) The Constitution also specifies the rights and duties of the citizens of the country.

The Constitution additionally serves a larger purpose: that of unifying the country. In a culturally, economically and socially diverse country like India, it brings about a sense of uniformity, as the set of rules and principles for governance enshrined in the Constitution of India applies to all Indians equally. The Constitution creates an identity for the country and its citizens. It tells us the kind of country India is or aspires to be. It explains the fundamental nature of our society.

Now the question is why do we need to know about these rules and principles? Let me give you an analogy. When we buy a new gadget, say, a mobile phone or a TV, we usually get a user manual along with it. The user manual tells us what features it offers, how the features can be activated, what can be done to rectify a problem if one encounters any, and what care should be taken to make it work properly. If you are not aware of the features, you may not be able to make full use of the product and may also end up doing something you should not have done. If you do not take proper care of it, it may stop working before it should have.

In the same way, the Constitution of India helps us understand our country better. If you are not aware of your rights and duties, you may end up doing something you should not have done. Similarly, if you do not know your rights, you would not know what to do if a wrong is done to you.

WHAT IS THERE IN THIS BOOK?

In this book, my research team and I have sifted through many books and other resources to compile relevant facts and structured them in ways that will make understanding the Constitution and Parliament of India easier and reading enjoyable.

We have divided the book into two broad sections—(*a*) the Constitution and (*b*) Parliament—for easy reference. As the aim of the book is to give a bird's eye view of the Constitution of India and the Indian Parliament, we have deliberately kept the entries short and crisp, without getting into too much detail. We have also tried to explain complex concepts as simply as possible.

Each entry comes with a 'Good to Know' section that contains interesting pieces of information related to the topic. There is also a glossary of terms to make understanding easier. In addition to these sections, we have also given appendices with relevant information.

This subject is very close to my heart and writing this book has been a rewarding experience. I would like to thank my research team—Ammar Hamid, Anik Ghosal, Ayashman Dey, Devarshi Ghosh, Natasha Gasper and Srirupa Roy—for their commendable work. I hope reading the book will be an enjoyable experience for you!

SECTION A
THE CONSTITUTION OF INDIA

THE MAKING OF THE CONSTITUTION—THE CONSTITUENT ASSEMBLY

The Constituent Assembly was a body of people entrusted with the task of drafting the Constitution of India. It was created in response to a demand by the Indian National Congress in the 1930s. Although the demand had been insistent, the British finally paid heed to it only after the outbreak of World War II (1939), when they found themselves amidst major financial crises. They tried to distance themselves from the affairs of India and allowed the Indians to take the lead in framing the Constitution of India.

The Constituent Assembly was an elected body of people, representing different parts of the country. It originally had 389 members. (At that time, British India, comprising the territories of modern-day India, Pakistan and Bangladesh, was made of two categories of territories: *a*) Provinces that were controlled directly by British officials, like Governors or Chief Commissioners, who were appointed by the Viceroy. These were Ajmer-Merwara, Assam, Baluchistan, Bengal, Bihar, Bombay, Central Provinces and Berar, Coorg, Delhi, Madras, the Northwest Frontier, Orissa, Punjab and the United Provinces. *b*) More than 500 princely states that were ruled by local hereditary rulers or jagirdars, who were allowed to run the internal affairs of their territories in return for acknowledging British sovereignty.)

This number decreased to 299 after the partition of the country as some members of the Constituent Assembly of India shifted to the Constituent Assembly of Pakistan.

The first meeting of the Constituent Assembly was held in New Delhi on 9 December 1946, under the temporary chairmanship of Sachchidananda Sinha. In less than seven weeks, it adopted the Objectives Resolution, moved by Jawaharlal Nehru, summarising the aims and objectives of the Assembly. Later that year, a Drafting Committee was set up under the chairmanship of B. R. Ambedkar to prepare the draft Constitution of India. While working on it, the Constituent Assembly proposed and discussed 7,635 amendments of which they rejected nearly 2,500.

The Constitution of India was adopted on 26 November 1949 and it came into force on 26 January 1950, exactly twenty years after the first Purna Swaraj Day was observed. The date 26 January 1930 had a great significance, as leaders and revolutionaries from across the country had come together to mark this special day as Complete Independence Day.

SESSIONS OF THE CONSTITUENT ASSEMBLY

First Session:	9–23 December 1946
Second Session:	20–25 January 1947
Third Session:	28 April–2 May 1947
Fourth Session:	14–31 July 1947
Fifth Session:	14–30 August 1947
Sixth Session:	27 January 1948
Seventh Session:	4 November 1948–8 January 1949
Eighth Session:	16 May–16 June 1949
Ninth Session:	30 July–18 September 1949
Tenth Session:	6–17 October 1949
Eleventh Session:	14–26 November 1949

On 24 January 1950, the members of the Constituent Assembly met to append their signatures to the Constitution of India.

GOOD TO KNOW
- Although India became independent in 1947, its Constitution came into force only in 1950. The first elected Lok Sabha (Lower House of the Parliament) and the first Rajya Sabha (Upper House of the Parliament) were constituted in 1952.
- The Constitution Hall, where the first meeting of the members of the Constituent Assembly was held, is now a part of the Parliament House.
- The date on which the Constitution of India was adopted (26 November 1949) is now observed in India as Law Day.
- The Constituent Assembly took two years, eleven months and seventeen days to draft the Constitution for independent India.
- As soon as India became independent, the Constituent Assembly started functioning as the Legislative Assembly of the newly formed country.

Glossary
▶ Draft: is a preliminary version of a written piece.

THE OBJECTIVES RESOLUTION

Here is the Objectives Resolution moved by Jawaharlal Nehru on 13 December 1946:

1. This Constituent Assembly declares its firm and solemn resolve to proclaim India as an Independent Sovereign Republic and to draw up for her future governance a Constitution;
2. Wherein the territories that now comprise British India, the territories that now form the Indian states, and such other parts of India as are outside British India and the

Contd.

states as well as such other territories as are willing to be constituted into the Independent Sovereign India, shall be a Union of them all; and

3. Wherein the said territories, whether with their present boundaries or with such others as may be determined by the Constituent Assembly and thereafter according to the law of the Constitution, shall possess and retain the status of autonomous units, together with residuary powers and exercise all powers and functions of government and administration, save and except such powers and functions as are vested in or assigned to the Union, or as are inherent or implied in the Union or resulting therefrom; and

4. Wherein all power and authority of the Sovereign Independent India, its constituent parts and organs of government, are derived from the people; and

5. Wherein shall be guaranteed and secured to all the people of India justice, social, economic and political: equality of status, of opportunity, and before the law; freedom of thought, expression, belief, faith, worship, vocation, association and action, subject to law and public morality; and

6. Wherein adequate safeguards shall be provided for minorities, backward and tribal areas, and depressed and other backward classes; and

7. Whereby shall be maintained the integrity of the territory of the Republic and its sovereign rights on land, sea and air according to justice and the law of civilized nations; and

8. This ancient land attains its rightful and honoured place in the world and makes its full and willing contribution to the promotion of world peace and the welfare of mankind.

THE MAKING OF THE CONSTITUTION—SELECT PEOPLE INVOLVED

B. R. AMBEDKAR

Bhimrao Ramji Ambedkar, a prominent leader of the freedom movement, is often referred to as the primary architect of the Indian Constitution. He played an important role in the drafting of the Constitution of India and after the country became independent, he served as its first Law Minister. He was awarded the Bharat Ratna posthumously in 1990.

B. R. Ambedkar was born on 14 April 1891, in Mhow (in present-day Madhya Pradesh), in a low-caste family and had to face discrimination throughout his life. Ambedkar studied at Elphinstone High School and Elphinstone College in Bombay (now called Mumbai). He graduated in Political Science and Economics from the University of Bombay (now called University of Mumbai) in 1912. In 1913, he went to study at Columbia University, New York, on scholarship. He received a PhD in Economics and later went to England. There, he studied at the London School of Economics and at Gray's Inn (to qualify as a barrister).

After returning to India in 1923, he started his legal practice in the Bombay High Court. While working as a lawyer, he devoted a lot of time to discussing social issues associated with the depressed classes and taking them to the right political forum. In 1927, he led a satyagraha in Mahad in Maharashtra, to ensure that the depressed classes got the right to draw water from the public Chavder tank. In 1930, he also started a movement at Kalram Temple, Nasik, to fight for the right of the Untouchables to enter the temple. In 1936, Ambedkar founded the Independent Labour Party and in 1942, he had the distinction of becoming the first Untouchables to be nominated to the Viceroy's Executive Council as the Minister of Labour.

His reputation as a scholar led to his appointment as the Chairman of the Drafting Committee on 29 August 1947. The draft Constitution prepared by him had a number of provisions ensuring the smooth functioning of the country and its institutions. It gave India a parliamentary form of government and guaranteed its citizens a wide range of rights, including the freedom to practise any religion. It provided for the abolition of untouchability, ensuring equality of all classes. Ambedkar argued in favour of far-reaching economic and social rights for women. He was a progressive thinker and felt that the provisions of the Constitution should be amendable to meet the demands of a nation that was in the process of evolution.

After India became independent, B. R. Ambedkar served as the first Law Minister of the country. He breathed his last on 6 December 1956. Less than two months before his death, he converted to Buddhism along with many other Untouchables.

GOOD TO KNOW
- A teacher in his school in Satara changed Bhimrao's surname Ambavadekar to Ambedkar.
- Nagpur, Maharashtra, has an international airport named after B. R. Ambedkar.
- Ambedkar's memorial in Mumbai is called Chaitya Bhoomi.

- His autobiography is entitled *Waiting for a Visa*.
- A district in Uttar Pradesh was named after Ambedkar in 1995 in recognition of his contribution to the cause of the depressed classes.

Glossary
- Satyagraha: was a concept that was introduced by Mahatma Gandhi to refer to a method of protest/resistance that was non-violent in nature. Literally meaning 'zeal for truth', this method was extensively used during the Indian struggle for freedom.
- Untouchable: is a term that was used for a person born into certain low castes.

JAWAHARLAL NEHRU

Jawaharlal Nehru was one of the greatest leaders of the Indian nationalist movement. When India became independent, he served as its first Prime Minister. For his services to the nation, Nehru was conferred the Bharat Ratna in 1955.

Nehru was born in Allahabad on 14 November 1889. The only son of Motilal Nehru and Swarup Rani, he was educated in England at Harrow, Cambridge and the Inner Temple. After completing his education in the UK, he returned to India and was deeply inspired by Mahatma Gandhi's thoughts and views. In 1919, he joined the Indian National Congress. In 1923, he became the General Secretary of the All India Congress Committee and founded the Independence for India League a few years later. He served as President of the historic Lahore session of the Indian National Congress in 1929, where the goal of 'complete independence' was adopted. At the Congress session in Bombay in 1942, he moved the 'Quit India' resolution.

Nehru was an integral part of the Constituent Assembly. During the term of his membership, he moved various resolutions including those on provisional adoption of Central Legislative Assembly rules and standing orders, the inclusion of Sikkim and Bhutan within the scope of the negotiating committee and the reports of the States Committee. He also performed one of the most important tasks of the newly constituted Assembly—moving the Objectives Resolution.

Nehru was a prolific writer; his many books include *Glimpses of World History* (1934), *The Discovery of India* (1946) and *Towards Freedom* (1958). He is often affectionately referred to as Chacha Nehru by children and his birth anniversary is celebrated across India as Children's Day.

GOOD TO KNOW
- In August 1942, Jawaharlal Nehru was imprisoned at the Ahmednagar Fort. It is considered his longest (nearly three years) and last confinement.
- In September 1946, an interim government of undivided India was formed under the leadership of Nehru.
- Nehru firmly believed in the doctrine of socialism. He also played a key role in the creation of the Non-alignment Movement.
- The Government of India instituted the Jawaharlal Nehru Award for International Understanding in 1965 to honour people for their outstanding contribution in promotion of international understanding, goodwill and friendship among people of the world.
- Shyam Benegal directed the TV series *Bharat Ek Khoj*, based on *The Discovery of India*.

Glossary
- Socialism: is a political or economic theory according to which the means of production, distribution and exchange should be owned or regulated by the community as a whole.
- Non-alignment Movement: was a movement in which some countries agreed to be 'non-aligned' to either of the two superpowers of the time—the USA and the erstwhile USSR.

MAULANA ABUL KALAM AZAD

Maulana Abul Kalam Azad was one of the most prominent leaders of the Indian freedom struggle. He was also a renowned scholar, poet and debater, living up to his name, Abul Kalam, which literally means 'Lord of dialogue'. He represented the ideas of secularism and unity in India. After India became independent in 1947, he served as its first Education Minister. He was posthumously awarded the Bharat Ratna in 1992.

Azad was born on 11 November 1888 in Mecca and came to India when he was young. He received his early education from his father at home. Later he was greatly inspired by the educationist Syed Ahmad Khan. Azad joined the Indian freedom struggle after he came in contact with two leading revolutionaries from Bengal—Aurobindo Ghose and Shyam Sundar Chakravarty. He joined the Indian National Congress in 1920 and was elected President of the special session of the Congress in Delhi a few years later. He was jailed a number of times.

Azad was an active member of the Constituent Assembly, representing the United Provinces. In the debates of the Assembly, he often spoke on issues related to the minorities in India. He believed that the communal problem in the country could only be resolved if the consent of all the affected parties was taken into consideration. He was a member of a committee that was entrusted with the task of discussing the distribution of seats with the Negotiating Committee.

As Education Minister in independent India (1947–58), Azad appointed the University and the Secondary Education Commissions, re-organised the All India Council for Technical Education and established the University Grants Commission and the Indian Institute of Technology, Kharagpur. He passed away on 22 February 1958. Azad's birth anniversary is celebrated as National Education Day in India.

> **GOOD TO KNOW**
> - Maulana Abul Kalam Azad was well-versed in many languages including Arabic, English, Urdu, Hindi, Persian and Bengali.
> - Film actor Aamir Khan's grandmother was Azad's niece.
> - Azad's book *India Wins Freedom* gives a detailed account of the freedom struggle of India.
> - Jawaharlal Nehru referred to Maulana Azad as Mir-i-Karawan or the caravan leader.
> - Each year, the Maulana Abul Kalam Azad Trophy is awarded by the President of India to a university for the all-round best performance in sports.

Glossary
▶ Bharat Ratna: is the highest civilian award in India.

RAJENDRA PRASAD

Rajendra Prasad was a freedom fighter and lawyer from Bihar who later became the first President of independent India. He was also the President of the Constituent Assembly. He received the Bharat Ratna in 1962 for his contribution to the nation.

Rajendra Babu, as he was popularly called, was born on 3 December 1884 in Zeradei, Bihar. He attended the Chhapra

Zilla School and then went to Calcutta (now called Kolkata) to do his M.A. from the University of Calcutta. During his college days, he joined the Dawn Society and was inspired by the teachings of Sister Nivedita, Surendra Nath Banerjee and many others. The Partition of Bengal in 1905 affected him deeply and led to the founding of the Bihari Students' Conference, a few years later. After studying law, Prasad practised in the Calcutta High Court and joined the Indian National Congress in 1911. Although he shifted to Patna in 1916 to practise law in the Patna High Court, he gave it up so that he could participate more actively in the Indian freedom struggle. Prasad's meeting with Gandhiji in 1917 in Bihar during the Champaran Movement was a turning point in his life. It inspired him to play an important part in the Champaran Satyagraha in Bihar, which led to the formulation of the Champaran Agrarian Act, in favour of the tenants in indigo plantations. In 1939, he became the President of Congress after Subhas Chandra Bose had resigned.

Prasad was elected as the President of the Constituent Assembly in 1946. He had a firm belief in the democratic process and ensured the participation of all its members before arriving at a decision. In order to ensure meaningful discussions in the House, he circulated reports to members well in advance, so that they could study them and contribute effectively. Prasad offered constructive views in the debates of the House. He was the Chairman of a number of committees in the Constituent Assembly including the Steering Committee and the Finance and Staff Committee. He addressed numerous issues including those related to the minorities.

After India became a republic, Prasad became the first President of the country. He passed away on 28 February 1963 at Bihar Vidyapeeth in Patna. He is chiefly remembered for his remarkable organisational capability and leadership qualities.

GOOD TO KNOW
- Rajendra Prasad was widely known as Deshratna.
- Prasad was deeply influenced by the principles of Mahatma Gandhi and wrote a book entitled *Bapu Ke Kadmon Mein* (1954).
- The autobiography of Prasad is entitled *Atmakatha* (1946).
- Prasad is the only President of India to have been elected twice to the post.

Glossary
- Agrarian: relates to cultivated land or the cultivation of land.
- Indigo: is a tropical plant which was widely cultivated as a source of dark blue dye.
- Republic: is a State in which supreme power is held by the people and their elected representatives.

SARDAR VALLABHBHAI PATEL

Sardar Vallabhbhai Patel, sometimes called the 'Bismarck of India', was a prominent leader during the Indian freedom struggle. He went on to hold different ministries in the first cabinet of independent India. He served as the Deputy Prime Minister and was in charge of the Ministry of Home Affairs, the Ministry of Information and Broadcasting, and the Ministry of States. He was posthumously awarded the Bharat Ratna in 1991.

Born on 31 October 1875 at Nadiad, Gujarat, Patel passed his matriculation examination from the Nadiad High School and became a lawyer by taking the Pleader's Examination. Later, he went to London and joined the Middle Temple. He returned to India in 1913 and started practising as a barrister in Ahmedabad. A few years later, Patel became a Municipal Councillor and then the Chairman of the Municipal Committee.

Mahatma Gandhi's leadership during the Champaran Satyagraha (1917) inspired Patel deeply and kindled his interest in politics. One of the landmark years in his life was 1928 when he led the villagers of Bardoli in a protest against increase in land revenue. His success in this satyagraha earned him the title of 'Sardar'. Patel presided over the 46th session of the Indian National Congress and continued to contribute significantly to the nationalist movement.

As Chairman of the Advisory Committee on Fundamental Rights, Minorities and Tribal and Excluded Areas, he presented a report on Fundamental Rights, clause by clause, and stressed on the necessity of dividing the Fundamental Rights into justiciable and non-justiciable rights. He also discussed provisions related to the states, the Union, citizenship, nationality, untouchability and non-discrimination.

After India gained independence, he played a crucial role in the integration of the princely states into the Union of India. He passed away on 15 December 1950.

GOOD TO KNOW
- The international airport in Ahmedabad is named after Sardar Vallabhbhai Patel.
- Paresh Rawal played the role of Patel in the 1993 film *Sardar*.
- After meeting Mahatma Gandhi, Patel took to spinning the charkha, boycotted foreign goods and clothes, and burned his foreign possessions in public bonfires.
- In 1965, the Indian Posts and Telegraphs Department issued a special commemorative stamp on Patel to observe his ninetieth birth anniversary.
- Patel is popularly known as the Iron Man of India because of his success in the integration of princely states after independence.

Glossary

- Pleader's Examination: was an examination that could enable one to become a lawyer.
- Justiciable right: is a type of right provided by the Constitution of India. If such a right is violated, a person can approach a court for redressal.
- Middle Temple: is one of the four associations for barristers in the United Kingdom.

SAROJINI NAIDU

Sarojini Naidu was a freedom fighter, political activist, feminist, poet-writer and the first Indian woman to become President of the Indian National Congress in 1925. She is often referred to as the 'Nightingale of India' on account of her beautiful poems and songs.

Born Sarojini Chattopadhyay on 13 February 1879 in Hyderabad, she was a brilliant student and topped the matriculation examination. Sarojini received her higher education from King's College, London, and later from Girton College, Cambridge. At the age of fifteen, she married Govindarajulu Naidu, a doctor, at a time when inter-caste marriages were not encouraged. It was a revolutionary step.

Naidu began her political career in 1906, inspired by the ideas of Gopal Krishna Gokhale, Rabindranath Tagore, Annie Besant and Mahatma Gandhi. In the following years, she actively participated in some of the most important campaigns in India like the Civil Disobedience Movement (1930–34) and the Quit India Movement (1942–44).

In the months leading to the independence, Naidu played an important role as a member of the Constituent Assembly. In various debates, she asked for an inclusive Constituent Assembly and put forward a resolution regarding the national flag.

After independence, Naidu became the first woman to become the Governor of an Indian state. She died in office two years later in March 1949. She was a prolific author and some of her works include *The Golden Threshold* (1905), *The Bird of Time* (1912), *The Sceptred Flute* (1928) and *The Feather of the Dawn* (1961).

> **GOOD TO KNOW**
> - Sarojini Naidu was awarded the 'Kaiser-e-Hind' medal by the British, for her work during the 1928 plague epidemic in India.
> - Naidu was well-versed in Urdu, Telugu, English, Bengali and Persian.
> - *Palanquin Bearers* is one of the most famous poems written by Naidu.
> - The tragic Jallianwala Bagh Massacre shocked her so much that Naidu gave up writing poems after the incident.
> - In her letters to Mahatma Gandhi, Naidu once referred to him as Mickey Mouse.

Glossary
▶ Palanquin: is a mode of transport consisting of a box carried on the shoulders of four or six bearers.

VIJAYA LAKSHMI PANDIT

Vijaya Lakshmi Pandit was an Indian freedom fighter, feminist, diplomat and politician. In 1953, she was the first woman to be elected President of the United Nations General Assembly.

Born to Motilal Nehru and Swarup Rani on 18 August 1900 in Allahabad, Uttar Pradesh, Vijaya Lakshmi Pandit was originally named Swarup Kumari Nehru. After receiving education in India and abroad, she became actively involved in the freedom struggle and was imprisoned thrice by the British. She became a member of the Legislative Assembly of the United Provinces and served as the Minister for Local Self-Government and Public Health in 1937.

As a member of the Constituent Assembly, Pandit spoke on topics like the centrality of New Asia that would emerge after India attained independence. After independence, she held a succession of high positions, including ambassadorships to the United States, Mexico and Britain and, in 1953, the presidency of the United Nations General Assembly. She served as the Governor of Maharashtra from 1962 to 1964, and became a member of Parliament soon after. In 1977, Pandit left the Congress Party to join Congress for Democracy, a political party founded that year. She passed away on 1 December 1990 at the age of ninety.

GOOD TO KNOW
- Vijaya Lakshmi Pandit was Jawaharlal Nehru's sister.
- The well-known novelist Nayantara Sahgal is Pandit's daughter.
- Pandit wrote the book entitled *The Scope of Happiness: A Personal Memoir*.
- In 1967, Pandit contested the Lok Sabha elections from the Phulpur parliamentary constituency in Uttar Pradesh and won.
- In 1979, she was appointed the Indian representative to the UN Human Rights Commission.

Glossary
- Feminist: is a person who advocates women's rights on the ground of gender equality.
- Diplomat: is the term for an official representing a country abroad.

OTHER LEADERS

The Constitution of India was the outcome of the efforts of a large number of people. Although these members came from culturally diverse backgrounds, represented different regions and held varied political thoughts, they were united in their aim of framing a Constitution that would provide its people equality and liberty. The members debated, discussed and amended each provision that eventually became a part of the great document. Sachchidananda Sinha, Pandit Govind Ballabh Pant, K.M. Munshi, Alladi Krishnaswamy Iyer, T.T. Krishnamachari and Sucheta Kripalani were some of the other prominent leaders. Apart from these members, there were some other people who played a crucial role in the drafting process. Among them were B.N. Rau, the Constitutional Adviser, and S.N. Mukherjee, the Chief Draftsman.

GOOD TO KNOW
- Many members of the Constituent Assembly went on to hold important cabinet portfolios in independent India. Rajkumari Amrit Kaur, one such member, joined the Central Cabinet as the Minister for Health.
- Govind Ballabh Pant, an important member of the Constituent Assembly received the Bharat Ratna in 1957.
- In the Constituent Assembly, Jammu and Kashmir was represented by Sheikh Muhammad Abdullah.
- Meira Kumar, the first woman Speaker of the Lok Sabha, is the daughter of Babu Jagjivan Ram, a member of the Constituent Assembly.
- After independence, Sardar Baldev Singh, a member of the Constituent Assembly of India, became the first Defence Minister of India.
- N. Sanjiva Reddy, a member of the Constituent Assembly, later went on to serve as the sixth President of India.

SOME WOMEN MEMBERS OF THE CONSTITUENT ASSEMBLY

1. **Ammu Swaminathan** (Constituency: Madras)
Subject spoken on
- Fundamental Rights and Directive Principles—the twin pillars of the Constitution

2. **Annie Mascarene** (Constituency: Travancore and Cochin Union)
Subjects spoken on
- Provincial elections
- Timetable for the House

3. **Begum Aizaz Razul** (Constituency: United Provinces)
Subjects spoken on
- Election to Council of States
- Fundamental Rights and Minority Rights
- Electoral system
- India's membership of the Commonwealth
- Powers of Parliament and the President

4. **Dakshyani Velayudan** (Constituency: Madras)
Subjects spoken on
- Forced labour
- Reservations for Harijans
- Draft Constitution: imprint of the Government of India Act, 1935

5. **G. Durgabai** (Constituency: Madras)
Subjects spoken on
- Appointment of judges of Provincial High Courts
- High Courts in newly created provinces
- The Constitutional Remedies for Fundamental Rights

Contd.

- Protection of children and youth from exploitation and abandonment
- The Supreme Court: guardian of the Constitution

6. **Hansa Mehta** (Constituency: Bombay)
Subjects spoken on
- Social, economic and political justice for women in India
- National flag
- Responsibility of the people in making the Constitution work

7. **Purnima Banerjee** (Constituency: United Provinces)
Subjects spoken on
- Qualifying age for membership of the State Legislature
- Relevance of the Upper House
- Finances for local bodies
- Electoral college for the Upper House of Provincial Legislature

8. **Renuka Ray** (Constituency: West Bengal)
Subjects spoken on
- Equality of status and justice for women
- Question of religious minorities and majorities in a secular state

9. **Sarojini Naidu** (Constituency: Bihar)
Subjects spoken on
- Seeking an inclusive Constituent Assembly
- Resolution regarding the national flag

10. **Sucheta Kripalani** (Constituency: United Provinces)
Subject spoken on
- Vande Mataram

11. **Vijaya Lakshmi Pandit** (Constituency: United Provinces)
Subject spoken on

Contd.

- Growth of Asia after the independence of India

12. **Kamala Chaudhuri** (Constituency: United Provinces)
Subject spoken on
- National flag

13. **Rajkumari Amrit Kaur** (Constituency: Central Provinces and Berar)
Subject spoken on
- National flag

THE CONSTITUTION—ITS FEATURES, STRUCTURE AND PROVISIONS

THE BOOK AND ITS SALIENT FEATURES

The Constitution of India is the very foundation on the basis of which India is governed. It is believed to be the lengthiest Constitution in the world. The original document had 395 Articles and eight Schedules. Here are some of the features of our Constitution:

1. The architects of the Constitution collected the best features of other existing constitutions and modified them to suit the needs of India. They adopted the features of the parliamentary system of government from the UK, the concept of Fundamental Duties from the erstwhile USSR and the idea of Directive Principles of State Policy from Ireland. Fundamental Rights, another important feature of our Constitution, was adopted from the Constitution of the USA.

2. The Constitution empowers Parliament to modify its provisions by legislation, if such a need is felt. Hence, it is flexible. This is evident from the fact that the Constitution has been amended a record ninety-eight times from 1951 to 2013.

3. The Constitution of India follows a federal system of

government with a unitary bias. In a federal system, political authority is divided between two independent sets of governments: national and sub-national. Generally, the national government exercises authority over the whole country while the sub-national government exercises independent control over smaller divisions of the country. Russia, Canada, USA, Brazil and Australia are some of the countries that follow this system. In a unitary system, on the other hand, most or all of the governing power rests with a centralised government. Most countries in the world follow the unitary system, including Great Britain, Japan, France, Poland, the Netherlands, Romania, Spain and many African countries.

In the case of India, political authority is divided between the central authority (for the whole country) and state authorities (for each constituent state), as in all federal governments. However, the government at the Centre can acquire the strength of a unitary system under certain conditions, as in the case of an Emergency. This is reinforced by the fact that there is a provision of single citizenship unlike in many federal countries which offer dual citizenship—one for the country and the other for the constituent unit.

4. The Constitution of India lays down the provisions for both the Union and the states, and not just for the Union.
5. The supremacy of the Constitution is one of its important features. No law can be made against its provisions.
6. The Constitution of India states that India is a secular State. It does not recognise any particular religion as its official religion and no discrimination can be made in India on grounds of religion.
7. Although India has a federal system, it has an integrated

judiciary. There is just one system of courts which handles cases both for the Union and the states instead of two different systems. Although the High Courts exercise powers in the states, the ultimate power rests in the hands of the Supreme Court of India.

> **GOOD TO KNOW**
> - Unlike India, the United Kingdom does not have a definite written document which they refer to as the Constitution of the UK. The Constitution of the UK is often described as 'partly written and wholly uncodified'.
> - Although Mahatma Gandhi played a major role in the freedom struggle, he was not alive when the Constitution of India finally came into force. The original version was signed by all the members of the Constituent Assembly in January 1950.
> - Jawaharlal Nehru was the first person to sign the Constitution of India. His son-in-law, Feroze Gandhi, was the last person to sign it.
> - The famous artist Nandalal Bose, along with some other artists, designed and decorated the original Constitution of India. The original Constitution of India was handwritten by Prem Behari Narain Raizada in his own impeccable calligraphy.
> - The original Constitution of India is kept in a special nitrogen-filled case in the library of the Parliament of India.

Glossary
▶ Calligraphy: is the art of writing using decorative letters.

STRUCTURE OF THE CONSTITUTION OF INDIA: ARTICLES, PARTS AND SCHEDULES

The Constitution of India deals with many topics like citizenship, elections, courts, Fundamental Rights and official languages. It starts with the Preamble, a kind of introduction to the book and is followed by twenty-two broad heads called Parts containing more than 350 Articles. There are twelve Schedules containing lists and other provisions. The structure is hereunder.

Parts	Contents	Articles
PART I	The Union and Its Territory	1–4
PART II	Citizenship	5–11
PART III	Fundamental Rights	12–35
PART IV	Directive Principles of State Policy	36–51
PART IVA	Fundamental Duties	51A
PART V	The Union	52–151
PART VI	The States	152–237
PART VII	The States in Part B of the First Schedule	238 (Repealed)
PART VIII	The Union Territories	239–242
PART IX	The Panchayats	243–243-O
PART IXA	The Municipalities	243P–243ZG
PART X	The Scheduled and Tribal Areas	244–244A
PART XI	Relations between the Union and the States	245–263
PART XII	Finance, Property, Contracts and Suits	264–300A

Contd.

PART XIII	Trade, Commerce and Intercourse within the Territory of India	301–307
PART XIV	Services under the Union and the States	308–323
PART XIVA	Tribunals	323A–323B
PART XV	Elections	324–329A
PART XVI	Special Provisions relating to Certain Classes	330–342
PART XVII	Official Language	343–351
PART XVIII	Emergency Provisions	352–360
PART XIX	Miscellaneous	361–367
PART XX	Amendment of the Constitution	368
PART XXI	Temporary, Transitional and Special Provisions	369–392
PART XXII	Short Title, Commencement, Authoritative Text in Hindi and Repeals	393–395

GOOD TO KNOW

- There are some provisions in the Constitution of India that have not been used so far. Article 360, dealing with Financial Emergency, which arises when the financial stability and credibility of the nation or any of its states is threatened, is one such example.
- Granville Austin, an American historian, was a leading authority on the Constitution of India. He has written two important books on the history of the Constitution of India: *The Indian Constitution: Cornerstone of a Nation* and *Working a Democratic Constitution: The Indian Experience*.

Glossary
- Repealed: is a term that refers to a law that is no longer in force

Each Article of the Constitution of India discusses a particular topic. Here are a few Articles:

> **A FEW ARTICLES OF THE CONSTITUTION OF INDIA**
>
> - Article 1 deals with the name and territory of the Union.
> - Article 356 deals with the failure of the constitutional machinery in the states. This is commonly referred to as President's Rule.
> - Article 370 deals with the temporary provisions with respect to the state of Jammu and Kashmir. It grants J&K a special autonomous status.
> - Article 17 deals with the abolition of untouchability.

PREAMBLE TO THE CONSTITUTION

The Preamble lays down the national goals, and states the aims and ideals of the nation. The Objectives Resolution of the Constituent Assembly is the basis of the Preamble to the Constitution.

The Preamble states:

WE, THE PEOPLE OF INDIA, having solemnly resolved to constitute India into a SOVEREIGN SOCIALIST SECULAR DEMOCRATIC REPUBLIC and to secure to all its citizens:
JUSTICE, social, economic and political;
LIBERTY of thought, expression, belief, faith and worship;
EQUALITY of status and of opportunity;

and to promote among them all
FRATERNITY assuring the dignity of the individual and the unity and integrity of the Nation;
IN OUR CONSTITUENT ASSEMBLY this twenty-sixth day of November, 1949, do HEREBY ADOPT, ENACT AND GIVE TO OURSELVES THIS CONSTITUTION.

The Preamble begins with the words 'We, the people of India...', which establishes the fact that the Constitution was created by the people of the country for themselves, through representatives and that the ultimate authority rests with the people. It strives to make India into a nation that is:

1. Sovereign (free from the control of any external power and having the authority to frame its own laws);
2. Socialist (working towards the welfare of its people);
3. Secular (not having an official state religion);
4. Democratic republic (run by representatives elected by the people, for their own welfare), in order to provide justice, liberty, equality and fraternity to all its citizens.

OTHER PREAMBLES

The following is often referred to as the Preamble to the Constitution of the USA:

'We the People of the United States, in Order to form a more perfect Union, establish Justice, insure domestic Tranquility, provide for the common defence, promote the general Welfare, and secure the Blessings of Liberty to ourselves and our Posterity, do ordain and establish this Constitution for the United States of America.'

GOOD TO KNOW

- Unlike many countries, India is a secular country having no State religion. The foremost religion of Sri Lanka is Buddhism, while Islam is the official religion in Malaysia.
- *The Republic* is a famous book by Plato, an ancient Greek philosopher and mathematician. In it, he attempted to interpret the concept of justice. Our Preamble, too, aims to secure justice for all its citizens and has underlined its relevance in social, economic and political spheres.
- US President Abraham Lincoln's Gettysburg Speech (19 November 1863) included the famous words: '...that government of the people, by the people, for the people, shall not perish from the earth. It defined the very concept of democracy.
- In Latin, the word 'preamble' means 'going or walking before'.
- The concepts of liberty, equality and fraternity were inspired by the Constitution of France.
- K. M. Munshi, a member of the Drafting Committee, referred to the Preamble as the 'Political Horoscope'.

THE UNION AND ITS TERRITORY

According to the Constitution, the entire territory of India includes three types of areas *a*) states *b*) union territories *c*) acquired territories. Article 1 of the Constitution of India states that India, that is Bharat, is a Union of states. This 'Union of states' refers to the twenty-nine member states as of 2014. The Parliament, by law, may admit into the Union, or create new states under certain terms and conditions. It may establish a new state by *a*) separating a territory from any existing state; *b*) combining two or more states or parts of states; *c*) uniting any territory to a part of any state. It may also increase or decrease the area of any state and change the name or boundary of any state.

> **GOOD TO KNOW**
> - Although the Constitution of India provides for the Constitution for both the Union and states, Jammu and Kashmir is the only state that was allowed to make its own Constitution (Article 370).
> - After independence, to make administration easier, many states were created on the basis of the language spoken in the region. In 1956, Andhra Pradesh became the first state to be created on the basis of language. It was followed by Kerala (for speakers of Malayalam), Karnataka (for speakers of Kannada), Maharashtra (for speakers of Marathi) and Gujarat (for those who had Gujarati as a mother tongue).
> - Sikkim, which was ruled by the Chogyal Dynasty, became a state of India in 1975.
> - Three states came into being in the year 2000: Chhattisgarh, Uttarakhand (then called Uttaranchal) and Jharkhand.
> - When the Constitution of India was adopted, the United Provinces was renamed as Uttar Pradesh.
> - Telangana became the twenty-ninth state of India in 2014.
> - Territory of India is an expression that is different from 'Union of India'. While the Union includes only the states, the 'Territory of India' includes the states along with all the union territories or any acquired territory that are a part of India.

Glossary
▶ Acquired territories: are those territories that India may acquire by purchase, treaty or conquest.

CITIZENSHIP

A citizen is a legally recognised member of a country who enjoys all the civil and political rights granted by it. The Constitution of India grants certain rights and privileges only to its citizens. These include:

1. the eligibility to hold certain offices such as those of the President of India, the Governor of a state and judge of the Supreme Court;
2. the right to become a member of Parliament;
3. the right to vote to the House of the People, the Legislative Assembly of a state, etc.

At the commencement of this Constitution, a person was considered a citizen if he/she was domiciled in India and ordinarily a resident in the territory of India for at least five years. The Constitution of India provides for single citizenship. There are different ways in which the citizenship of India can be acquired or lost.

The citizenship of India can be acquired in the following ways:

1. Birth
2. Descent
3. Registration
4. Naturalisation
5. Incorporation of territory

According to the Citizenship Act, 1955, citizenship of India can be lost by termination, deprivation and renunciation. It can be terminated if a person renounces his/her citizenship or acquires the citizenship of another country. The Central Government has the power to deprive any citizen of India of this right if it feels that his/her being a citizen is not in the best interests of the country. If a citizen of India, who is also a citizen or national of another country, formally gives up his/her Indian citizenship, he/she will cease to be a citizen of India.

According to the Amendment of the Citizenship Act, 1955, Persons of Indian Origin, who are now citizens of another country, are eligible to be granted Overseas Citizenship of India (OCI) except in the case of Pakistan and Bangladesh.

> **GOOD TO KNOW**
> - Mother Teresa was born on 26 August 1910 as Agnes Gonxha Bojaxhiu in Skopje, Macedonia (in Europe). She adopted Indian citizenship in 1948.
> - Pravasi Bharatiya Divas or Non-resident Indian Day is celebrated on 9 January every year, in honour of the overseas Indian community which plays an important role in the growth of India. The day commemorates Mahatma Gandhi's return to India from South Africa on 9 January 1915.
> - Several Nobel Laureates were born in India but were citizens of other countries when they received the Nobel Prize. For example, S. Chandrashekhar and Hargobind Khorana were citizens of USA when they received the Nobel Prize.
> - A passport is an official document that is issued by a government, stating the holder's identity, including his/her citizenship, entitling the holder to travel to other countries.

Glossary

- Renunciation: is the official announcement by a person that he or she does not own, support or believe in something any longer.
- Naturalisation: is becoming a citizen of another country

under certain conditions.
- Descent: is the origin of a person in terms of family.

TYPES OF PASSPORTS

Three types of passports are issued in India. These are:

Regular Passport: It has a navy blue cover and is issued to an Indian citizen for ordinary travel, that is, for holidays and business trips. It is valid for ten years from the date of issue and can be renewed for another ten years.

Diplomatic Passport: It has a maroon cover and is issued to Indian diplomats and high-ranking government officials.

Official Passport: It has a grey cover and is issued to people representing the Indian government on official business abroad.

FUNDAMENTAL RIGHTS AND FUNDAMENTAL DUTIES

Fundamental Rights are a list of rights given in Part III of the Constitution. These are included to protect the interests of a person and to ensure social, economic and political justice for all. While all the rights are available to Indian citizens, only a few are available to foreigners, for example, equality before the law, protection of life and personal liberty, freedom of religion and right against exploitation.

The six Fundamental Rights are:

1. Right to Equality
2. Right to Freedom
3. Right against Exploitation
4. Right to Freedom of Religion
5. Cultural and Educational Rights
6. Right to Constitutional Remedies

The difference between a Fundamental Right and any other right provided by the Constitution is that if the Fundamental Right of a person is violated, he can directly appeal to the Supreme Court of India for redressal, but in the case of infringement of any other right, he has to approach other courts. The Supreme Court can issue writs (formal written orders) of *Habeas corpus, Mandamus, Certiorari, Prohibition* and *Quo warranto*, to restore a Fundamental Right.

WRITS

Certiorari: is a writ meaning 'to be certified'. It is issued by the Supreme Court to lower courts or tribunals ordering them to transfer the matter to a superior authority to ensure proper consideration.

Habeas corpus: is a Latin word literally meaning 'you shall have the body (in court)'. It is issued by the court to a person who has detained another person. The court orders him to bring the detained person before it and to explain the reason why he has been detained. If the person has been wrongly confined, the court can let him go.

Mandamus: is a Latin word meaning We Command. It is an order from a superior court to a lower court or tribunal or public authority, to perform an act, which is a part of its duty.

Prohibition: is a writ that is issued by a superior court to a lower court or a tribunal when the lower court tries to perform an act that is not within its jurisdiction.

Quo warranto: is a word literally meaning 'by what warrants?' It is issued by the court to a person who asserts a claim to a public office to which he is not entitled.

In addition to these rights, there are certain duties of every citizen of the country, in order to uphold the sovereignty, unity and integrity of the nation and foster the feeling of brotherhood among the people. These are called Fundamental Duties. Although these duties are very important, they are not enforceable by the Constitution. The Fundamental Duties of every citizen of India are to:

1. abide by the Constitution and respect its ideals and institutions, the national flag and the national anthem;
2. cherish and follow the noble ideals which inspired our national struggle for freedom;
3. uphold and protect the sovereignty, unity and integrity of India;
4. defend the country and render national service when called upon to do so;
5. promote harmony and the spirit of common brotherhood amongst all the people of India transcending religious, linguistic and regional or sectional diversities; to renounce practices derogatory to the dignity of women;
6. value and preserve the rich heritage of our composite culture;
7. protect and improve the natural environment including forests, lakes, rivers and wildlife, and to have compassion for living creatures;
8. develop the scientific temper, humanism and the spirit of inquiry and reform;
9. safeguard public property and to abjure violence;
10. strive towards excellence in all spheres of individual and collective activity so that the nation constantly rises to higher levels of endeavour and achievement;
11. provide opportunities for education to one's child or, as the case may be, ward between the age of six and fourteen years. (This Fundamental Duty was added to the Indian

Constitution by 86th Amendment to the Constitution in 2002.)

> **GOOD TO KNOW**
> - The Right to Property was a Fundamental Right till 1978 and then it ceased to be so and was converted into an ordinary legal right. It was inserted as Article 300A in Part XII which deals with finance, property, contracts and suits
> - B. R. Ambedkar called the Right to Constitution Remedies, 'the very soul of the Constitution and the very heart of it'.
> - According to Right Against Exploitation, any child below the age of fourteen cannot be employed in any factory or engaged in any other hazardous employment.
> - Jawaharlal Nehru referred to the Fundamental Rights relating to equality and liberty, as the 'conscience of the Constitution'.

Glossary
- Infringement: means the violation of a law or right.

DIRECTIVE PRINCIPLES OF STATE POLICY

The Directive Principles of State Policy are an important part of our Constitution. Although they are not enforceable by law, it is the duty of the Government of India to consider these principles while making laws and apply them in administration.

To ensure the social, economic and political welfare of the people, the government shall make policies in such a manner that both men and women get an equal opportunity to earn their livelihood and receive equal pay. The ownership and control of the material resources of the community are distributed in such a way that it ensures common good and does not lead to the concentration of wealth in the hands of a few people. The government shall aim at improving the working conditions and the standard of life of workers, and make effective provisions for handling unemployment, old age and sickness.

Some of the other directives include protection of national monuments, promotion of justice on the basis of equal opportunity, provision of free legal aid, organisation of village panchayats, proclamation of a uniform civil code for the whole country, and protection and improvement of the environment.

> **GOOD TO KNOW**
> - At different points in time, governments at the Centre have launched national-level programmes or schemes for the welfare of the people in accordance with the Directive Principles of State Policy, for example, the National Rural Employment Programme and the National Rural Health Programme schemes.

THE UNION EXECUTIVE: THE PRESIDENT OF INDIA

The President of India is the Constitutional Head of the Republic of India and all executive actions are taken in his name. He is the first citizen of the country and does not represent any political party. He is elected through an Electoral College consisting of the elected members of the

1. Lok Sabha and the Rajya Sabha;
2. Legislative Assemblies of the states and
3. Legislative Assemblies of the union territories of Puducherry and Delhi.

For a person to be qualified for election as President, he/she must be a citizen of India, must be at least thirty-five years of age and should have the qualification for election as a member of the House of the People. He must not hold any office of profit including those under the Government of India or the government of any state. The President is elected for a term of five years commencing from the date on which he enters upon his office and he is also eligible for re-election. Before entering upon his office, the President swears an oath of affirmation in the presence of the Chief Justice of India. The President can be removed from his position by a process called impeachment. If the President wishes to resign, then he needs to address a letter to the Vice President of India.

The President has many executive powers. He appoints the Prime Minister and other ministers on the advice of the Prime Minister. Certain top officials including the Chief Justice of India, Governors of states, the Chief Election Commissioner, the Comptroller and Auditor General of India and the Attorney General of India, are also appointed by him.

The President is the supreme commander of the armed forces of India (Indian Army, Indian Navy, Indian Air Force), and has the power to declare war or conclude peace, if approved by the Parliament.

The President has many parliamentary functions. He can summon the sessions of both Houses of Parliament, either separately or jointly. He addresses both Houses of Parliament assembled together, at the beginning of the first session every year. After each General Election to the Lok Sabha, he addresses the members at the commencement of the first session. He also has the power to dissolve the Lok Sabha.

The President's role in law making is crucial as a Bill does not become an Act unless he gives his stamp of approval. After a Bill is passed by the two Houses of Parliament, it is presented to the President who either signs it or withholds his assent. If it is not a Money Bill, he may send it back to the Houses for reconsideration. But once the Bill is returned, it is obligatory for him to give his assent. A Money Bill can only be introduced in the Lok Sabha on the recommendation of the President of India.

If the President of India feels that there is a circumstance where he needs to take immediate action and parliamentary enactment on the subject is not possible, he can legislate by Ordinances.

Under the Constitution, a Bill related to the Consolidated Fund of India can only be passed by either House of Parliament if the President has recommended it. The reports of the Auditor General, Finance Commission, Union Public Service Commission such other organisations are submitted to the President, who then causes them to be laid before each House of Parliament. He is also responsible for the laying out of the Union Budget before Parliament. Any advance that needs to be made out of the Contingency Fund of India, in order to meet any unforeseen expenditure, has to be approved by him.

The President of India also has great pardoning power. He can grant pardon, substitute a form of punishment with another (of a lighter character), reduce the term of sentence and award a lesser sentence instead of a penalty in dealing with matters to which the executive power of the Union extends. Most important of all, he is the only person who can pardon a sentence of death.

Even though a great number of powers are vested in the President, in actual practice, he does not have too much control over matters as he is bound to act in accordance with the advice of the Council of Ministers.

GOOD TO KNOW
- The Retreat Building in Shimla and the Rashtrapati Nilayam in Hyderabad are the two official retreats of the President of India.

- The President's Bodyguard is the oldest regiment of the Indian Army. It is a cavalry unit and was raised as early as 1773 by the then Governor General, Warren Hastings.
- A pair of railway coaches, numbered 9000 and 9001, is reserved for the President of India. Built in 1956 for the President's travels, it is popularly called the Presidential Saloon.
- The official residence of the President of India, the Rashtrapati Bhavan, is in New Delhi.

Glossary
- The Attorney General of India: is the first law officer of the Government of India. He gives advice to the President of India on legal matters.
- The Comptroller and Auditor General of India: is the head of the audit and accounts system of India and controls the financial system of the country at the state and the Union levels.
- Office of profit: refers to an official position that brings to the holder some financial gain, benefit or advantage.
- Electoral College: is a body of electors chosen by a larger group.

SHORT BIOGRAPHIES OF PRESIDENTS OF INDIA

Here is a short introduction to all the people who have served as the President of India (in chronological order):

*Rajendra Prasad (26 January 1950–13 May 1962)**

Rajendra Prasad was the first President of India. He was born on 3 December 1884 in Bihar and was educated in Bihar and

---

*The dates within brackets denote the tenure of each President.

Calcutta. He actively participated in the freedom struggle and served as the President of the Constituent Assembly of India from 1946 to 1949. After India became a republic in 1950, he served as the country's first President. Throughout his life, he maintained a very simple lifestyle.

Rajendra Prasad was awarded the Bharat Ratna in 1962. He passed away in 1963.

Sarvepalli Radhakrishnan (13 May 1962–13 May 1967)

Born on 5 September 1888 at Tiruthani (Tamil Nadu), Sarvepalli Radhakrishnan was educated in Tirupati, Vellore and Madras. He became the Vice Chancellor of Andhra University in 1931 and was the Indian Ambassador to the USSR from 1949 to 1952. He became the first Vice President of India in 1952 before becoming the President of India in 1962.

Radhakrishnan's birthday is celebrated as 'Teachers' Day' across India. He received the Bharat Ratna in 1954 and the British knighthood in 1931.

Zakir Husain (13 May 1967–3 May 1969)

Zakir Husain was born in 1897 in Hyderabad. He served as the Vice Chancellor of two major institutions of India: Jamia Millia Islamia and Aligarh Muslim University. He served as the Governor of Bihar from 1957 to 1962 and was the Vice President of India 1962 to 1967. Zakir Husain became the President of India in 1967 and held the office till his death in 1969.

He was awarded the Padma Vibhushan in 1954 and the Bharat Ratna in 1963.

Varahagiri Venkata Giri (3 May 1969–20 July 1969, Acting President)

Check on next page.

Justice Mohammed Hidayatullah (20 July 1969–24 August 1969, Acting President)

Born on 17 December, 1905, Justice Hidayatullah became the Acting President of India by virtue of his position as the Chief Justice of India. He became the Acting President when the then President of India, Zakir Husain suddenly died and the office of the Vice President, too, fell vacant. (When Zakir Husain died, the then Vice President V.V. Giri was made the acting President; however he resigned from the post to take part in the presidential elections and so Justice Hidayatullah was made the Acting President.) Justice Hidayatullah became the President so as the Constitution directs the Chief Justice of India to become the President of India if the positions of both the President and the Vice President fall vacant.

He has received numerous awards including the Order of the British Empire in 1946. He passed away in 1992.

Varahagiri Venkata Giri (24 August 1969–24 August 1974)

V. V. Giri was born on 10 August 1894 in Berhampur (in present-day Odisha), and studied in Madras and Ireland. He served as a minister in Madras before being appointed as the Indian High Commissioner to Ceylon (currently Sri Lanka) (1947–51). In the following years, he served as the Governor of Uttar Pradesh, Kerala and the erstwhile Mysore state. V.V. Giri became the Vice President of India in 1967 before occupying the highest chair in the country two years later.

He was a prolific writer and a good orator. He was awarded the Bharat Ratna in 1975 and passed away in 1980.

Fakhruddin Ali Ahmed (24 August 1974–11 February 1977)

Fakhruddin Ali Ahmed was born on 13 May 1905 in Delhi. He studied History at the University of Cambridge and law at the

Inner Temple in London. Later, while serving as the Minister of Finance and Revenue of Assam (1938), he was responsible for some radical taxation measures. He became a Union Minister in 1966 when Prime Minister Indira Gandhi included him in her first cabinet.

Fakhruddin Ali Ahmed was sworn in as the President of India in 1974 and continued in the office till his death in 1977.

B. D. Jatti (12 February 1977–24 July 1977, Acting President)
Basappa Danappa Jatti was born on 10 September 1912. He served as the Lieutenant Governor of Pondicherry (now called Puducherry) and the Governor of Orissa (now called Odisha) before becoming the Vice President of India in 1974.

In 1977, B. D. Jatti became the Acting President of India for a period of around five months following the death of Fakhruddin Ali Ahmed. He passed away in 2002.

Neelam Sanjiva Reddy (25 July 1977–25 July 1982)
Neelam Sanjiva Reddy was born on 19 May 1913 in Elluru in Ananthapur (Andhra Pradesh). He was educated in Madras (now called Chennai) before he gave up his studies to join the freedom struggle.

In 1956, he became the first Chief Minister of Andhra Pradesh and went on to serve as a Union Minister and also as Speaker of the Lok Sabha in subsequent years. He had the rare distinction of becoming the first President of India to be elected unanimously. He passed away in 1996.

Giani Zail Singh (25 July 1982–25 July 1987)
Giani Zail Singh was born on 5 May 1916 in Punjab. He served as a member of the Rajya Sabha from 1956 to 1962 and became the Chief Minister of Punjab in 1972. In 1980, he became the

Union Home Minister and went on to become the President of India two years later. He passed away in 1994 following a car crash.

R. Venkataraman *(25 July 1987–25 July 1992)*

Born on 4 December 1910 in the Thanjavur district (Tamil Nadu), R. Venkataraman studied Law at the University of Madras and began practising law in 1935. He actively participated in the freedom struggle and was jailed by the British (1942–44), and after India became independent, he held many important positions. He was in charge of various ministries in the state government of Madras before becoming a member of the Planning Commission.

In 1980, R. Venkataraman became a Union Minister and held the Finance and Defence portfolios. He occupied the chair of the Vice President of India from 1984–87 before becoming the President of India in 1987, a position he held till 1992. He passed away in 2009.

Shankar Dayal Sharma *(25 July 1992–25 July 1997)*

Shankar Dayal Sharma was born in Bhopal on 19 August 1918 and received his doctorate in Law from Cambridge University. He, like many of his predecessors, actively participated in the freedom struggle. He served as the Chief Minister of the erstwhile Bhopal State and Governor of Andhra Pradesh, Punjab and Maharashtra. Before becoming the Vice President in 1987 and President in 1992, he had served as a legislator and parliamentarian for more than two decades.

Shankar Dayal Sharma wrote a large number of articles on different subjects in various national and international journals. He passed away in 1999.

K. R. Narayanan (25 July 1997–25 July 2002)

K. R. Narayanan was born in present-day Kerala. He obtained an M.A. degree in English Literature standing first in the University of Travancore and obtained a degree in Economics from the London School of Economics. After returning to India, he joined the Indian Foreign Service in 1949 and served as the Indian ambassador to Thailand, Turkey, China and the United States of America. He became Secretary to the Ministry of External Affairs in 1976 and was appointed Vice Chancellor of the Jawaharlal Nehru University in 1979, a post he held till 1980. Before becoming the President of India in 1997, he served as the Vice President of the country from 1992 to 1997.

K. R. Narayanan was associated with several institutions in diverse capacities. He was a scholar and a prolific writer having authored several books and contributed many articles to diverse publications. K. R. Narayanan was once described by Jawaharlal Nehru as 'the best diplomat of the country'. He passed away in 2005.

A. P. J. Abdul Kalam (25 July 2002–25 July 2007)

Born on 15 October 1931 in Rameswaram, Tamil Nadu, A. P. J. Abdul Kalam studied Aeronautical Engineering at the Madras Institute of Technology and joined Hindustan Aeronautics Limited (HAL) at Bangalore (now called Bengaluru) as a trainee. He worked with various organisations including the Indian Space Research Organisation (ISRO), Defence Research & Development Organisation (DRDO) and the Department of Atomic Energy (DAE) before becoming the President of India.

As a scientist, A. P. J. Kalam contributed significantly to the development of India's first indigenous Satellite Launch Vehicle (SLV-III). He also played an important role in the development and functioning of Agni and Prithvi missiles.

A. P. J. Kalam went on to become the Scientific Adviser to the Defence Minister and during this period he led the projects for strategic missile systems. He also monitored the Pokhran-II nuclear tests in collaboration with the Department of Atomic Energy, which gave a boost to India's nuclear capabilities. In 2002, A. P. J. Kalam was sworn in as the President of India.

A. P. J. Kalam, one of the most remarkable scientists of our time, has received honorary doctorates from numerous universities and institutions. He has been awarded the Padma Bhushan (1981), Padma Vibhushan (1990) and the Bharat Ratna (1997). A prolific author, he has written many bestselling books including *Wings of Fire, Ignited Minds* and *My Journey*. He has taken a keen interest in igniting young minds by interacting with them across the country so that they can contribute to the development of the country.

Pratibha Devisingh Patil (25 July 2007–25 July 2012)
Pratibha Patil was born on 19 December 1934 in Maharashtra. She obtained a degree in Law from the Government Law College in Mumbai. Patil contributed actively towards the welfare of women, children and the poor. She went on to serve as a Rajya Sabha member from 1985 to 1990, and was elected as a Lok Sabha member in 1991. She was the Governor of Rajasthan when she was appointed as the first woman President of the country.

Pranab Mukherjee (25 July 2012–till date)
Pranab Mukherjee was born on 11 December 1935 in West Bengal. His father was a freedom fighter and a Congress leader. He studied History, Political Science and Law before teaching at a college and working as a journalist. He started active political life in 1969 after becoming a member of the Rajya Sabha.

In the following years, Pranab Mukherjee held various

important positions in the union ministry. He became Finance Minister of India for the first time in 1982 and was Leader of the House in the Rajya Sabha from 1980 to 1985. Later, he served as Deputy Chairman of the Planning Commission from 1991 to 1996, Minister for Commerce from 1993 to 1995, Minister of External Affairs from 1995 to 1996, Minister of Defence from 2004 to 2006 and once again the Minister of External Affairs from 2006 to 2009.

Pranab Mukherjee was the Minister of Finance from 2009 to 2012 and Leader of the Lok Sabha from 2004 to 2012 when he resigned to contest the election to the office of the President. He was a member of the Congress Working Committee, the party's highest policy-making body for a period of twenty-three years.

Pranab Mukherjee has received many awards and honours including the Padma Vibhusan in 2008, the Best Parliamentarian Award in 1997 and the Best Administrator in India Award in 2011.

GOOD TO KNOW
- 'Thinking should become your capital asset, no matter whatever ups and downs you come across in your life', is a famous quote by A. P. J. Abdul Kalam.
- Pratibha Patil was a table tennis champion during her college days and was also instrumental in organising the Women's Home Guard in the Jalgaon district.
- Rajendra Prasad served as the President of India for the longest duration.
- N. Sanjiva Reddy was the youngest President of India, so far, at the time of appointment.
- In 2004, A. P. J. Abdul Kalam became the first Indian President to visit the Siachen Glacier—the highest battlefield in the world.

THE UNION EXECUTIVE: THE VICE PRESIDENT OF INDIA

The Vice President of India is the second highest constitutional office in India. The Vice President is not a member of either House of Parliament. He is elected by the members of an Electoral College consisting of members of both Houses of Parliament, for a period of five years. If the office of the President falls vacant due to death, illness, resignation or removal, the Vice President carries out the functions of the President until a new President is elected. In order to be qualified for election as a Vice President, a person must be a citizen of India, be at least thirty-five years of age and must not hold any office of profit. He should also be qualified for election to the Council of States. He should also meet the eligibility criteria as those required by a person to become a member of the Rajya Sabha.

As the Vice President of India, he serves as the ex-officio Chairman of the Rajya Sabha. But when the Vice President serves as the President of India, he stops functioning as the ex-officio Chairman of the Rajya Sabha.

VICE PRESIDENTS OF INDIA	
Name	Term of Office
S. Radhakrishnan	13.5.1952 to 12.5.1962
Zakir Husain	13.5.1962 to 12.5.1967
V.V. Giri	13.5.1967 to 3.5.1969
Gopal Swarup Pathak	31.8.1969 to 30.8.1974
B.D. Jatti	31.8.1974 to 30.8.1979
M. Hidayatullah	31.8.1979 to 30.8.1984
R. Venkataraman	31.8.1984 to 24.7.1987
Shankar Dayal Sharma	3.9.1987 to 24.7.1992
K. R. Narayanan	21.8.1992 to 24.7.1997
Krishan Kant	21.8.1997 to 27.7.2002
Bhairon Singh Shekhawat	19.8.2002 to 21.7.2007
Mohammad Hamid Ansari	11.8.2007 till date

> **GOOD TO KNOW**
> - So far, no woman has served as the Vice President of India.
> - After S. Radhakrishnan, Mohammad Hamid Ansari is only the second Vice President of India to be re-elected for a second term.

Glossary

▶ Ex-officio: is a term often used for such a member of a body who holds the position because he/she occupies another designated office.

THE UNION LEGISLATURE: PARLIAMENT OF INDIA

The Parliament of India is discussed in detail in Section B of this book.

THE STATE EXECUTIVE: THE GOVERNOR

The executive power of a state in India rests with the Governor. He is the constitutional head of the state. All executive actions of the state are taken in his name.

The Governor of a state is not elected but is appointed by the President of India and holds his office during the pleasure of the President. A person can serve as the Governor of more than one state at a time. The normal term of a Governor's office is five years. The oath of the Governor is administered in the presence of the Chief Justice of the High Court.

A citizen of India who is at least thirty-five years of age is eligible for the post. He must not be a member of the legislature of the Union or of any state and he must not hold any office of profit.

The Governor has legislative (related to the legislature), judicial (related to the administration of justice) and executive (related to the implementation of laws) powers at the state level just like those of the President of India at the Union level. In certain cases, the Constitution of India gives the Governor the authority to use his 'discretionary power' while in most others, he acts on the advice of a Council of Ministers headed by the Chief Minister of the state.

The Governor makes several appointments. He appoints the Council of Ministers on the advice of the Chief Minister. The Advocate General and the members of the State Public Commission are also appointed by him. The ministers and the Advocate General hold office during the pleasure of the Governor.

Although the Governor does not have the power to appoint the Chief Justice and the judges of the High Court of the state, he has the right to be consulted by the President in the matter.

The Governor also has the power to nominate a member of the Anglo-Indian community to the Legislative Assembly of his state if they are not adequately represented in the Assembly. In a state where the legislature is bicameral, he can nominate 'persons having special knowledge or practical experience in respect of matters such as literature, science, art, co-operative movement and social service' to the Legislative Council.

He can address and send messages to the State Legislature, just as the President does in Parliament. The Annual Financial Statement is laid before the legislature on his instruction.

The Governor has the power to grant pardons, substitute a form of punishment with another (of a lighter character) and reduce the term of sentence of any person convicted of any crime relating to a matter to which executive power of the state extends.

Although the Governor does not have any emergency

powers, he can send a report to the President if he feels that a situation has arisen in which it is not possible for the state government to follow the provisions of the Constitution of India and requires imposing President's Rule.

If a Governor has to resign, he must submit his resignation to the President of India.

> **GOOD TO KNOW**
> - The official residence of the Governor of a state is called the Raj Bhavan.
> - Usually, the official vehicle of the Governor of a state has the national emblem in place of a number plate.
> - The Raj Bhavan in Kolkata used to be the residence of Governor Generals and Viceroys of India, and served as the seat of power in British India for over a century.
> - Many women have become Governors of states in India. Some of them include Sarojini Naidu, Padmaja Naidu, Vijaya Lakshmi Pandit, Sharda Mukherjee, Fathima Beevi, Margaret Alva and Sheila Dikshit.

Glossary
▸ Discretionary power: is the power or authority of a person to decide what should be done in a particular situation, and it is normally not dictated by rules.

THE STATE LEGISLATURE

The Constitution of India provides for a federal government. In a federal Constitution, the powers of the government are divided at two levels: for the whole country (Centre or Union) and for the states. The Constitution contains provisions for governance at both these levels. The pattern of government in the states is similar to that at the Centre. Both follow a parliamentary system with the executive head being the constitutional ruler.

While in most states of India, the legislature is unicameral, consisting of the Legislative Assembly only, in the rest, it is bicameral, consisting of two Houses, namely the Legislative Assembly (Vidhan Sabha) and the Legislative Council (Vidhan Parishad). The Legislative Council is called the Upper House while the Legislative Assembly is called the Lower House. There are provisions in the Constitution for the abolition or creation of the Legislative Council in a state.

The members of the Legislative Assembly (MLAs) of each state are chosen by direct election from different legislative constituencies in the state, just like the members of the Lok Sabha are elected from different parliamentary constituencies of India. The number of members of the Assembly cannot be more than 500 or less than sixty, with certain exceptions. The term of the Legislative Assembly is normally of five years and the Speaker is responsible for conducting business in the Assembly. For a person to be eligible for election to the Legislative Assembly, he should be at least twenty-five years of age, should be a citizen of India and possess qualifications as required by the Parliament.

In the Legislative Council, some members are indirectly elected and some are nominated or chosen by the Governor. The Legislative Council is not subject to dissolution, but one-third of its members retire at the end of every second year. The Chairman is responsible for conducting business in the Council. The eligibility criteria for election to the Legislative Council is the same as those for the Legislative Assembly except the age limit, which is thirty years.

The size of the Legislative Council depends on the strength of its Legislative Assembly. The size of the Legislative Council may vary, but its membership should not be more than one-third of the membership of the Legislative Assembly but not less than forty. The Legislative Assembly is more powerful than the Legislative Council.

> **GOOD TO KNOW**
> - In 1957, the state of Andhra Pradesh created a Legislative Council and then abolished it in 1985.
> - The Karnataka State Legislature is housed in an imposing building called the Vidhana Soudha. The words 'Government Work is God's Work' are inscribed on it.
> - The Ujjayanta Palace in Tripura, which once housed the royal family, also served as the seat of the State Legislature in later years.

The following table shows the list of different states and union territories of India, and the corresponding number of members in the Legislative Assembly and the Legislative Council (if it exists there):

STRENGTH OF STATE LEGISLATURES		
State / Territory	**Number of members in Legislative Assembly**	**Number of members in Legislative Council (if the state has a Legislative Council)**
Andhra Pradesh	175	50
Arunachal Pradesh	60	Nil
Assam	126	Nil

Contd.

Bihar	243	75
Chhattisgarh	90	Nil
National Capital Territory of Delhi	70	Nil
Goa	40	Nil
Gujarat	182	Nil
Haryana	90	Nil
Himachal Pradesh	68	Nil
Jammu and Kashmir	87	36
Jharkhand	81	Nil
Karnataka	224	75
Kerala	140	Nil
Madhya Pradesh	230	Nil
Maharashtra	288	78
Manipur	60	Nil
Meghalaya	60	Nil
Mizoram	40	Nil
Nagaland	60	Nil
Odisha	147	Nil
Punjab	117	Nil
Rajasthan	200	Nil
Sikkim	32	Nil
Tamil Nadu	234	Nil
Telangana	119	40
Tripura	60	Nil
Puducherry	30	Nil
Uttarakhand	70	Nil
Uttar Pradesh	403	100
West Bengal	294	Nil

COUNCIL OF MINISTERS AND THE CHIEF MINISTER

The Council of Ministers is a select group of members of the State Legislature which helps and advises the Governor. The Council of Ministers of a state is headed by the Chief Minister. While the Chief Minister is appointed by the Governor, the other ministers are appointed by the Governor on the advice of the Chief Minister. The Council of Ministers is collectively responsible to the Legislative Assembly.

The role of the Chief Minister of a state is similar to that of the Prime Minister in the Central Government. Both of them head their respective Council of Ministers. The Chief Minister presides over the meetings of the Council of Ministers and plays an important role in decision-making. He guides and coordinates the activities of all the ministers in his council. As he is the head of the Council of Ministers, his resignation or death automatically dissolves the cabinet.

He acts as the principal channel of communication between the Governor and the Council of Ministers. He advises the Governor with regard to the appointment of important officials like the Advocate General, Chairman and members of the State Public Service Commission, State Election Commissioner, and so on.

GOOD TO KNOW
- In India, many Chief Ministers have gone on to become the Prime Minister. They include Morarji Desai, Charan Singh, V.P. Singh, P.V. Narasimha Rao, H.D. Deve Gowda and Narendra Modi.
- In India, there have been many instances of both father and son serving as the Chief Minister. While Omar Abdullah, the former Chief Minister of Jammu and Kashmir, is the son of former Chief Minister Farooq Abdullah, Akhilesh

> Yadav is the son of the former Chief Minister of Uttar Pradesh, Mulayam Singh Yadav.
> - Sucheta Kripalani was the first woman Chief Minister of an Indian state (Uttar Pradesh).
> - In 2014, Pawan Kumar Chamling was sworn in as the Chief Minister of Sikkim for the fifth consecutive term.
> - Actor, Anil Kapoor played the role of a Chief Minister in the 2001 film *Nayak: The Real Hero*.
> - The record for the longest serving woman Chief Minister is held by Sheila Dikshit, the former Chief Minister of Delhi.

JUDICIARY

The judiciary is an organ that interprets laws and resolves disputes. It is often regarded as the guardian of the Constitution of India. It protects the interests of its citizens by providing justice in case of violation of a law or right.

The Constitution of India has provided for a single combined system of courts for the Union as well as the states, implementing both Union and state laws. The Supreme Court of India stands at the head of the entire system, followed by the High Courts at the state level. Below the High Courts are the subordinate courts.

These subordinate courts are divided into two branches: civil and criminal courts. While the civil courts have the authority to handle all kinds of civil disputes, the criminal courts handle criminal cases. At this level, the District Judge is the highest judicial authority in the civil court. He is followed by the Subordinate Judge and the Munsiff below him. The Sessions Judge is the highest judicial authority in the criminal court. He is followed by the Assistant Sessions Judge. At the bottom of the rung is the First Class Magistrate.

The Supreme Court is headed by the Chief Justice of India and consists of not more than thirty other judges. According to the Constitution of India, every judge of the Supreme Court is to be appointed by the President of India on the advice of his ministers and in consultation with the Chief Justice of India and such judges of the Supreme Court and of the High Courts in the states, as the President may deem fit.

The High Courts are headed by the Chief Justice of that particular High Court. Every judge of a High Court is appointed by the President in consultation with the Chief Justice of India, the Governor of the state, and, in the case of appointment of a judge other than the Chief Justice, the Chief Justice of the High Court.

The Constitution does not mention the terms of appointment of the Chief Justice of India. By convention, the senior-most judge of the Supreme Court is appointed as the Chief Justice of India. Although this tradition has been followed for most appointments, there have been exceptions.

In actual practice, appointments and transfers of Supreme Court judges are decided by a closed group comprising the Chief Justice of India and four senior-most judges of the Supreme Court. This is referred to as the collegium system. This system, with a slight variation, is also followed in the appointment of High Court judges.

In 2014, a Bill was passed in Parliament to make way for the setting up of a National Judicial Appointments Commission which will appoint and transfer judges to the Supreme Court and the High Courts in India. If the process is completed it will replace the collegium system.

For a person to be eligible for appointment as a judge of the Supreme Court he has to be *a*) a citizen of India and *b*) either be a distinguished jurist or someone who has been a

High Court judge for at least five years or has been an advocate of a High Court (or two or more such courts in succession) for at least ten years.

There is no minimum age criterion for appointment as a judge of the Supreme Court. There is no fixed term for a person to serve as a Supreme Court judge. He is entitled to hold his office till *a*) the age of sixty-five; *b*) he resigns by writing to the President; *c*) he is removed by the President through a process called impeachment whereby the members of Parliament vote for the removal of the judge.

For a person to be eligible for appointment as a judge of the High Court he has to *a*) be a citizen of India, not more than sixty-two years of age and *b*) have held a judicial office for not less than ten years in the territory of India or have practised as an advocate of a High Court (or two or more such courts in succession) for at least ten years. The judge of a High Court holds office until the age of sixty-two years.

> **GOOD TO KNOW**
> - The shape of the building of the Supreme Court of India is based on the image of the scales of justice. The central wing of the building acts as the central beam of the scales.
> - Leila Seth, mother of the famous author Vikram Seth, was the first woman to become the Chief Justice of a High Court in India. She was also the first woman judge of the Delhi High Court.
> - The states of Manipur, Tripura, Meghalaya and Nagaland are under the jurisdiction (High Court) of Assam.
> - The Andaman and Nicobar Islands are under the jurisdiction of the Calcutta High Court.

The following table shows the names of the persons who have served as the Chief Justice of India and their respective terms:

CHIEF JUSTICES OF INDIA

Chief Justices of India	Date of Appointment As C.J.I.	Held Office Till
1. Justice Harilal Jekisundas Kania	26/01/1950	06/11/1951
2. Justice M. Patanjali Sastri	07/11/1951	03/01/1954
3. Justice Mehr Chand Mahajan	04/01/1954	22/12/1954
4. Justice Bijan Kumar Mukherjea	23/12/1954	31/01/1956
5. Justice Sudhi Ranjan Das	01/02/1956	30/09/1959
6. Justice Bhuvneshwar Prasad Sinha	01/10/1959	31/01/1964
7. Justice P.B. Gajendragadkar	01/02/1964	15/03/1966
8. Justice A.K. Sarkar	16/03/1966	29/06/1966
9. Justice K. Subba Rao	30/06/1966	11/04/1967
10. Justice K.N. Wanchoo	12/04/1967	24/02/1968
11. Justice M. Hidayatullah	25/02/1968	16/12/1970
12. Justice J.C. Shah	17/12/1970	21/01/1971
13. Justice S.M. Sikri	22/01/1971	25/04/1973
14. Justice A.N. Ray	26/04/1973	28/01/1977
15. Justice M. Hameedullah Beg	29/01/1977	21/02/1978
16. Justice Y.V. Chandrachud	22/02/1978	11/07/1985
17. Justice P.N. Bhagwati	12/07/1985	20/12/1986

Contd.

18. Justice R.S. Pathak	21/12/1986	18/06/1989
19. Justice E.S. Venkataramiah	19/06/1989	17/12/1989
20. Justice Sabyasachi Mukherjee	18/12/1989	25/09/1990
21. Justice Ranganath Misra	25/09/1990	24/11/1991
22. Justice K.N. Singh	25/11/1991	12/12/1991
23. Justice M.H. Kania	13/12/1991	17/11/1992
24. Justice L.M. Sharma	18/11/1992	11/02/1993
25. Justice M.N. Venkatachaliah	12/02/1993	24/10/1994
26. Justice A.M. Ahmadi	25/10/1994	24/03/1997
27. Justice J.S. Verma	25/03/1997	17/01/1998
28. Justice M.M. Punchhi	18/01/1998	09/10/1998
29. Justice A.S. Anand	10/10/1998	31/10/2001
30. Justice S.P. Bharucha	01/11/2001	05/05/2002
31. Justice B.N. Kirpal	06/05/2002	07/11/2002
32. Justice G.B. Pattanaik	08/11/2002	18/12/2002
33. Justice V.N. Khare	19/12/2002	01/05/2004
34. Justice S. Rajendra Babu	02/05/2004	31/05/2004
35. Justice R.C. Lahoti	01/06/2004	31/10/2005
36. Justice Y.K. Sabharwal	01/11/2005	13/01/2007
37. Justice K.G. Balakrishnan	14/01/2007	11/05/2010
38. Justice S.H. Kapadia	12/05/2010	28/09/2012
39. Justice Altamas Kabir	29/09/2012	18/07/2013
40. Justice P. Sathasivam	19/07/2013	26/04/2014

Contd.

| 41. Justice R. M. Lodha | 27/04/2014 | 27/09/2014 |
| 42. Justice H.L. Dattu | 28/09/2014 | Till date |

UNION TERRITORIES

There are seven union territories in India namely National Capital Territory of Delhi, Andaman and Nicobar Islands, Lakshadweep Islands, Dadra and Nagar Haveli, Daman and Diu, Puducherry and Chandigarh. Unlike the states which have a Governor as the head, the union territories are administered by an administrator acting as an agent of the President. The Governor of a state may serve as the administrator of an adjoining union territory.

GOOD TO KNOW
- Barren Island, located in the Andaman and Nicobar Islands, is home to the only active volcano in India.
- The different regions of the union territory of Puducherry are scattered and do not share borders with each other. While Puducherry and Karaikal regions share exclusive land borders with Tamil Nadu, Mahe does so with Kerala and Yanam with Andhra Pradesh.
- Chandigarh is the capital of two states: Haryana and Punjab.
- Himachal Pradesh was the first union territory to become a state.
- The administrator of Delhi is designated as the Lieutenant Governor.

PANCHAYATS

The panchayat has been a unit of rural administration in India for many centuries. After independence, the government was dissatisfied with the weak functioning of the panchayat. There were numerous reasons behind this, including the absence of regular elections, insufficient representation of weaker sections like Scheduled Castes, Scheduled Tribes and women, and lack of financial resources. In order to address this issue and grant them the power and authority to function as effective units of self-government, the 73rd Amendment Act was passed in 1992. It led to the addition of Part IX to the Constitution of India. Some of the things it provided for were gram sabha in a village or group of villages, the formation of panchayats at village and other levels, and reservation of seats for the Scheduled Castes and Scheduled Tribes in proportion to their population for membership.

The term of each panchayat is five years from the date of its first meeting. The minimum age for a person to become a member of the panchayat is twenty-one years.

The panchayat is organised at three levels: *a*) village level; *b*) intermediate level and *c*) district level. All the seats are meant for persons chosen by direct election from territorial constituencies in the 'panchayat' area.

Zilla parishad is a local government body in India at the district level. Panchayat samiti is the link between the gram panchayat and the zilla parishad.

The panchayats play a very important part in rural administration. They may be entrusted with the task of *a*) preparing plans and carrying out schemes for economic and social development; *b*) working on matters related to education, land improvement and animal husbandry, among others.

GOOD TO KNOW

- Mahatma Gandhi once said about Indian villages: 'India lives in her villages, not in her cities.' He also said: 'If the village perishes, India perishes too.'
- The word 'panchayat' literally means council of five members.
- The 73rd Amendment Act added as many as sixteen Articles in relation to the establishment of and elections to the panchayats.

Glossary

- Zilla parishad: is a local government body in India at the district level. The Hindi word 'parishad' means council and 'zilla parishad' translates to district council.
- Panchayat samiti: is the link between the gram panchayat (village council) and the zilla parishad (district council).

MUNICIPALITIES

A municipality is an institution of self-government in urban areas. In India, these bodies have been in existence for a long time. Some of the earliest municipal corporations were set up in Madras and Calcutta in the seventeenth and eighteenth centuries. However, after independence, these local bodies gradually became weak and ineffective. This led the Parliament to enact the Constitution (73rd Amendment) Act, 1992 to help strengthen the functioning of the bodies as strong democratic units of self-governance. This Act came into force in 1993 and a new part relating to municipalities, was added to the Constitution. Some of the factors this Act provided for were a fixed duration of municipalities, appointment of state election commission, appointment of state finance commission and the formation of metropolitan and district planning committees.

There are three types of municipalities in every state: *a*) nagar panchayat for a transitional area (an area in transition from a rural area to an urban area); *b*) municipal council for a smaller urban area and *c*) municipal corporation for a larger urban area.

The legislatures of states may entrust them with the responsibility of preparation of plans for economic development and social justice, the implementation of schemes related to urban planning, regulation of land use, roads and bridges, water supply, public health, urban forestry, etc. They may also be authorised to levy, collect and appropriate certain taxes, duties, tolls and fees, etc.

Any person who is eligible to be chosen as a member of the State Legislature shall be qualified for being a member of a municipality, the only difference being the age limit, which is twenty-one years in this case.

Any municipality shall continue for a period of five years from the date of its first meeting and if it is dissolved before expiration of its term, elections are to be held within six months of its dissolution.

According to the Census of India, an urban area is defined as:

1. A place with a municipality, corporation, cantonment board or notified town area committee, etc.
2. All the places which satisfy the following criteria:
    i. A population of at least 5,000;
    ii. At least 75 per cent of the male working population engaged in non-agricultural pursuits;
    iii. A density of population of at least 400 persons per sq km.

GOOD TO KNOW
- Established on 29 September 1688, the Corporation of Madras (now known as Corporation of Chennai) is believed to be the oldest such institution in India. It was created on the advice of Josiah Child of the East India Company. He was inspired by the model of the Dutch government in the East Indies.
- The famous leader Subhas Chandra Bose was elected the Mayor of Calcutta on 22 August 1930.

Glossary
▸ Metropolitan: is a very large and busy city.

RELATIONS BETWEEN THE UNION AND THE STATES

The responsibility of governing this huge country has been divided between the Parliament and the State Legislatures. While Parliament can make laws for the whole or any part of the territory of India, the legislature of a state may make laws for the whole or any part of the state. Three lists have been created to ensure smooth functioning. These lists appear in the Seventh Schedule of the Constitution of India. The lists are:

1. Union List: Parliament has the sole power to make laws on matters on this list.
2. State List: The Legislature of a state has exclusive power to make laws on matters on the list. But, under certain conditions, Parliament too can make laws on matters given in this list.
3. Concurrent List: Parliament and legislature of any state have the power to make laws on matters on this list.

If the State Legislature and Parliament both make laws on a matter mentioned in the State List at a time when Parliament has been given the responsibility to do so (under Articles 249 and 250), the law made by Parliament shall be in effect till Parliament is in charge of this matter.

In case of an Emergency, Parliament shall have the right to make laws on matters given in the State List. (Also refer to Appendix 5 for an in-depth account of the three lists.)

> **GOOD TO KNOW**
> - The National Library, the Indian Museum, the Victoria Memorial, the Indian War Memorial and any other institution of similar stature that is financed by the Government of India and declared by Parliament by law, to be an institution of national importance, is a part of the Union List.

FINANCE

In order to carry out its duties, it is very important for the government to have sufficient financial resources at its disposal. The Constitution of India discusses issues related to finance, property, contracts and suits in great detail. It also makes provisions for, among other things, the distribution of taxes and non-tax revenues, the power of borrowing and provisions for grants-in-aid by the Union to the states. No tax can be levied or collected except by an authority of law.

The accounts of the Government of India are kept in the following ways:

1. Consolidated Fund of India: Any amount of money received by the Government of India through taxes (Income Tax, Central Excise), loans (from foreign governments and international institutions) and other transactions are credited into a fund called the Consolidated Fund of India. This fund

pays for the expenditure of the government. No amount can be withdrawn from the fund without authorization from Parliament.
2. Public Account of India: All other public money received by the government that is not included in the Consolidated Fund of India is credited to the Public Account of India.
3. Contingency Fund of India: This is a special fund used for meeting an unforeseen expenditure. The fund is periodically replenished from the Consolidated Fund of India.

> **GOOD TO KNOW**
> - Manmohan Singh is the only Prime Minister of India to have signed a banknote. He signed banknotes when he was Governor of the Reserve Bank of India, from 1982 to 1985.
> - The King's portrait on the coins of British India was replaced by the Lion Capital of the Ashoka Pillar on the first coins issued by the Republic of India on 15 August 1950.
> - The Contingency Fund of a state is placed at the disposal of its Governor.
> - The President of India appoints the Chairman of the Finance Commission of India. The first Finance Commission was constituted in 1951. It is constituted to give its recommendations to the President on financial matters such as distribution of the net proceeds of taxes between the Union and the states.

Glossary
▶ Suits: also known as lawsuits, are claims or disputes that are brought to a court of law for redressal.

SERVICES UNDER THE UNION AND THE STATES

In the parliamentary form of government, while the policies of administration are laid down by ministers, they are implemented by a large body of officials called civil servants. Unlike the ministers, who are chosen from the party in majority, these officials are appointed through a rigorous process of recruitment. They are trained in the art of administration and work without political bias, unlike the ministers. Such members hold office during the pleasure of the President in the case of the Union, and during the pleasure of the Governor in the case of the state, with certain exceptions.

An official of the Central Services works with the Central Government while an official of the State Services works with the state government. The officials of All India Services can serve either at the central level or the state level. The All India Services include the Indian Administrative Service (IAS), Indian Police Service (IPS) and the Indian Forest Service (IFS).

Parliament has the power to alter any condition of services including those related to remuneration, pension and disciplinary matters. The Union Public Service Commission (UPSC) or its counterpart in the state is consulted on all matters related to methods of recruitment for civil servants.

A member of the Union Public Service Commission serves for a period of six years or up to the age of sixty-five years, whichever is earlier.

GOOD TO KNOW
- The Dholpur House on Shahjahan Road in New Delhi houses the Union Public Service Commission.
- The Lal Bahadur Shastri National Academy of Administration in Mussoorie imparts training to all the recruits of civil services.

- The Sardar Vallabhbhai Patel National Police Academy is situated in Hyderabad. It trains officers of the IPS.

ELECTIONS

The responsibility of conducting elections in India rests with an independent body called the Election Commission of India. Established in 1950, it conducts elections to the offices of the President and Vice President of India, Parliament, State Legislative Assemblies and Legislative Councils. The Election Commission consists of a Chief Election Commissioner and Election Commissioners. The Chief Election Commissioner has a tenure of six years, or up to the age of sixty-five years, whichever is earlier.

The State Election Commissions are responsible for conducting elections to the corporations, municipalities, zilla parishads, district panchayats, panchayat samitis, gram panchayats and other local bodies in each state/union territory. They are independent of the Election Commission of India.

The elections to the Lok Sabha are on the basis of universal adult suffrage—every citizen of India, who is at least eighteen years of age and is not disqualified under the Constitution or by law for, among other things, being mentally unstable, practising criminal or illegal activities, or being a non-resident, is eligible to be registered as a voter at the General Elections.

The first General Elections to the Lok Sabha were held in 1951–52.

GOOD TO KNOW
- The National Voters' Day is observed on 25 January every year to mark the foundation day of the Election Commission of India.

- The headquarters of the Election Commission of India is located in New Delhi.
- The Chief Election Commissioner is mostly selected from the Indian Administrative Service (IAS).

CHIEF ELECTION COMMISSIONERS OF INDIA

Name	Took office on	Left office on
Sukumar Sen	21 March 1950	19 Dec 1958
Kalyan Sundaram	20 December 1958	30 September 1967
S.P. Sen Verma	1 October 1967	30 September 1972
Nagendra Singh	1 October 1972	6 February 1973
T. Swaminathan	7 February 1973	17 June 1977
S.L. Shakdhar	18 June 1977	17 June 1982
R.K. Trivedi	18 June 1982	31 December 1985
R.V.S. Peri Sastri	1 January 1986	25 Nov 1990
V.S. Ramadevi	26 November 1990	11 December 1990
T.N. Seshan	12 December 1990	11 December 1996
M.S. Gill	12 December 1996	13 June 2001
J.M. Lyngdoh	14 June 2001	7 February 2004
T.S. Krishnamurthy	8 February 2004	15 May 2005
B.B. Tandon	16 May 2005	29 June 2006
N. Gopalaswami	30 June 2006	20 April 2009
Navin Chawla	21 April 2009	29 July 2010
S.Y. Quraishi	30 July 2010	10 June 2012
V.S. Sampath	11 June 2012	15 January 2015
H.S. Brahma	16 January 2015	Till date

SPECIAL CLASSES

Special provisions have been made in the Indian Constitution with regard to certain classes. Through these, the Constitution has sought to protect the interests of socially and economically backward sections of the society, so that the ideals of equality and justice for all can be achieved. Seats are reserved for the Scheduled Castes and the Scheduled Tribes in the Lok Sabha in the same proportion which these particular sections represent in the total population of the state or the union territory. Similarly, in the Legislative Assemblies of the states, there is reservation of seats for the Scheduled Castes and the Scheduled Tribes in the aforementioned proportions. Also, the President of India may nominate to the Lok Sabha, not more than two members of the Anglo-Indian community, if he is of the opinion that the community is not adequately represented there.

The Constitution has also provided for appointments to services and posts in the Union or a state where members of the Scheduled Castes and the Scheduled Tribes can be considered, consistently with maintaining the efficiency of administration. The National Commission for Scheduled Castes and the National Commission for Scheduled Tribes have also been constituted to work towards the welfare of these sections. Additionally, the President may choose to appoint a Commission for safeguarding the interests of socially and educationally backward classes within the territory of India.

The Chairperson, Vice Chairperson and other members of the National Commission for Scheduled Tribes are appointed by the President.

GOOD TO KNOW
- Article 330 of the Indian Constitution provides for reservation of seats for Scheduled Castes and Scheduled Tribes in the Lok Sabha.
- The term OBC refers to Other Backward Classes, while the term EBC is sometimes used to refer to Economically Backward Classes.

OFFICIAL LANGUAGE OF INDIA

India, with more than a thousand languages, posed a major challenge to the makers of the Constitution of India when they set out to select one of its numerous languages as the official language of the country. Of the total number of languages, fourteen (presently twenty-two) were identified as major languages, in terms of the number of people using them. These languages are listed in the Eighth Schedule of the Constitution. As Hindi was the most commonly used language on this list, Hindi, in the Devanagari script, was made the official language of India. At the commencement of the Constitution, English, too, was allowed for all official transactions, for a period of fifteen years.

Although Hindi was recognised as the official language of India, the Constitution of India empowered the State Legislature to adopt any one or more of its native languages to be used for official purposes of that state. Until the State Legislature otherwise provided by law, English was allowed to be used for official purposes in the state. If there is a demand by the people of a particular state to recognise a local language as an official language, the President can issue directions for the same.

According to the Constitution of India, unless Parliament felt otherwise, English is the preferred language for all proceedings in the Supreme Court or High Courts and all Bills introduced in Parliament or State Legislatures. However, a State Legislature or the Governor may prescribe the use of any language, other than English, with certain exceptions. The Department of Official Languages in India is administered by the Ministry of Home Affairs.

The Eighth Schedule of the Constitution contains a list of twenty-two languages. There are two primary reasons for the creation of this list: *a*) to give representation to the members speaking these languages in the Official Languages Commission and *b*) to enrich Hindi with inputs from the given languages.

LANGUAGES IN THE EIGHTH SCHEDULE

1. Assamese
2. Bengali
3. Bodo
4. Dogri
5. Gujarati
6. Hindi
7. Kannada
8. Kashmiri
9. Konkani
10. Maithili
11. Malayalam
12. Manipuri
13. Marathi
14. Nepali
15. Odia
16. Punjabi
17. Sanskrit
18. Santhali
19. Sindhi
20. Tamil
21. Telugu
22. Urdu

GOOD TO KNOW
- The Constitution of India was adopted by the Constituent Assembly in English. A Hindi translation of the Constitution, bearing the signatures of the members of the Constituent Assembly, was published in 1950.

- According to the *Guinness Book of World Records*, South Africa has the maximum number of official languages—eleven. These are English, Afrikaans, isiZulu, isiXhosa, Sesotho, Setswana, Sepedi, Xitsonga, siSwati, isiNdebele and Tshivenda.
- According to the Constitution, every state would try to provide facilities for instruction in the mother tongue at the primary stage of education.
- Sanskrit is the second official language of Uttarakhand.
- Tamil is also an official language of Singapore.

EMERGENCY PROVISIONS

The term 'Emergency' is used to refer to the existence of a condition in which the security of India or any part of it is threatened by war or external aggression or armed rebellion. The Constitution provides for three different kinds of Emergencies: *a*) an Emergency due to war, external aggression or armed rebellion; *b*) Failure of constitutional machinery in the states; *c*) Financial Emergency. A Proclamation of Emergency is made by the President of India in consultation with the cabinet ministers headed by the Prime Minister.

Provisions related to Emergencies were modelled on the Constitution of Germany. The first proclamation of Emergency under Article 352 was made during the Indo-China War of 1962. A proclamation of Emergency was again made in India during Indira Gandhi's term on 25 June 1975 on the ground of 'internal disturbance'. It was revoked on 21 March 1977. A condition of a Financial Emergency may arise when financial stability and credibility of the nation or any of its states is threatened though this provision as mentioned in Article 360, has never been used.

GOOD TO KNOW
- By the 44th Amendment Act, 1978, the words 'armed rebellion' replaced the words 'internal disturbance'.

AMENDMENTS TO THE CONSTITUTION OF INDIA

In order to meet the demands of a newly independent nation, the makers of the Constitution, in Article 368, made provisions for its amendment. While most parts of the Constitution are changeable, any amendment that destroys, what is referred to as the 'basic structure' of the Constitution, is not acceptable and can be declared null and void by the court.

The usual process of amendment starts with the introduction of a Bill in either House of the Parliament. It has to be passed by a majority of the total membership of each House and by not less than two-third members present and voting. Once the Bill is passed by both the Houses it is presented to the President for his approval. After it is sanctioned by the President, it becomes a Constitutional Amendment. Although this method applies to most of the provisions, there are certain exceptions, including those related to the manner of election of the President of India and the extent of the executive power of the Union and the states. Any amendment to these Articles requires the approval of the legislatures of at least half of the states before it is presented to the President for his assent.

The First Amendment Act was enacted in 1951. The 42nd Amendment Act, 1976 is considered a milestone in the history of amendments as it introduced substantial changes in the Constitution. It introduced changes in the Preamble, and in more than fifty Articles and seven Schedules.

GOOD TO KNOW
- Sikkim became the twenty-second state of India with the enactment of the 36th Amendment Act, 1975.
- The 70th Amendment Act empowers the members of the legislatures of Delhi and Puducherry to be a part of the Electoral College for election of the President.

SOME AMENDMENTS MAKING BILLS INTO ACTS

The Constitution (24th Amendment) Act, 1971—It proposed to amend Articles 13 and 368 of the Constitution empowering Parliament with the authority to amend any provision of the Constitution. It also stated that if a Constitution Amendment Bill is presented to the President for his signature, he cannot withhold his assent. The Bill was introduced in the Lok Sabha on 28 July 1971. It was discussed on 3rd and 4th August and passed without any changes on 4 August 1971. The Bill, as passed by the Lok Sabha, was taken up by the Rajya Sabha on 10th and 11th August and passed by that House on 11 August 1971.

The Constitution (45th Amendment) Act, 1980—It was introduced in the Lower House of Parliament on 23 January 1980. It proposed to amend Article 334 in the Constitution of India with regard to provisions related to the reservation of seats for certain classes. The Bill was considered by the Lok Sabha on 24 January 1980 and passed on the same day in the original form. The Bill, as passed by the Lok Sabha, was considered and passed by the Rajya Sabha on 25 January 1980. This Act extended the period of the reservation of seats for the Scheduled Castes and the Scheduled Tribes and the representation of the Anglo-Indian community by

Contd.

nomination in the House of the People and in the Legislative Assemblies of the states for a further ten years.

The Constitution (61st Amendment) Act, 1988—It was introduced in the Lok Sabha on 13 December 1988 as the Constitution (62nd Amendment) Bill, 1988. The Bill sought to amend Article 326 of the Constitution by reducing the voting age of the citizens of India from twenty-one years to eighteen years. The Bill was considered by the Lok Sabha on 15 December 1988 and passed the same day. The Bill, as passed by the Lok Sabha, was considered and passed by the Rajya Sabha on 20 December 1988.

SECTION B
THE PARLIAMENT OF INDIA

THE PARLIAMENT HOUSE

The Constitution of India provides for a parliamentary system of government consisting of the President and two Houses known as the Rajya Sabha (Council of States) and the Lok Sabha (House of the People). The Parliament of India plays a significant role in the smooth functioning of the country. It is mainly responsible for:

1. creating and monitoring the Cabinet (a body of ministers responsible for controlling government policies);
2. making, amending and repealing laws;
3. handling the finances of the country.

The Parliament of India functions from the Parliament House in New Delhi.

The Parliament House Estate comprises the Parliament House, Reception Office building, Parliament Library Building, Parliament House Annexe and the extensive lawns around it. The two Houses of Parliament are located in, and function from the Parliament House, also called the Sansad Bhavan. The Parliament House also has the offices of important functionaries. It has twelve gates of which Gate no. 1 on the Sansad Marg (Parliament Street) is the main gate.

The Parliament House was designed by two famous architects Sir Herbert Baker and Sir Edwin Lutyens. The foundation stone was laid on 12 February 1921 and the entire structure was built over a period of nearly six years, at the cost of eighty-three lakh rupees. Built on an area of nearly six acres, it is a circular building. At its centre is the Central Hall. It has three horseshoe-shaped structures built around it: the Lok Sabha, the Rajya Sabha and the Library Hall, and in-between are open garden courts.

It was in the Central Hall of Parliament that the transfer of power from the British Crown to India took place on 15 August 1947. The Constituent Assembly met in this hall from 9 December 1946 to 26 November 1949 to frame our Constitution. Subsequently, the Constitution of India was also adopted in this historic hall.

The Parliament Library, located in the Parliament House Estate, is the second largest library in India, ranked after the National Library in Kolkata. Until 1958, the Supreme Court of India functioned from the Parliament House till it moved to its present location.

GOOD TO KNOW
- The Lok Sabha TV and the Rajya Sabha TV are television channels that show live telecasts of the proceedings from the respective houses of Parliament.
- The Parliament House appears on the reverse of the contemporary 50-rupee currency note in India.
- The Parliament House was originally known as Council House.
- The floor covering and furnishings of the Lok Sabha are green in colour, while those of the Rajya Sabha are maroon in colour.

SESSIONS OF PARLIAMENT
Normally, the following three sessions of Parliament are held in a year:
1. Budget Session: (February–May)
2. Monsoon Session: (July–August)
3. Winter Session: (November–December)

THE LOK SABHA

HISTORY, COMPOSITION AND TERM

The Lok Sabha is the Lower House of Parliament. It is called the popular chamber because its members are chosen by the people through direct election. It was constituted for the first time in April 1952, following the first General Elections. The first session of the First Lok Sabha started from 13 May 1952.

To become a member of the Lok Sabha, a person has to *a*) be a citizen of India; *b*) be at least twenty-five years of age; *c*) have all the other qualifications that may be prescribed by Parliament by law.

The maximum strength of the Lok Sabha is 552. Of this *a*) a maximum of 530 members are chosen by direct election from parliamentary constituencies across different states of India; *b*) a maximum of twenty members represent the union territories; *c*) a maximum of two members of the Anglo-Indian community are to be nominated by the President if he/she feels that the community is not adequately represented in the House. At present, the total number of Lok Sabha seats is about 545.

The outer limit on the maximum number of members chosen directly from constituencies in states may increase under certain circumstances, like in the case of reorganisation of states.

For the purpose of elections, the country is divided into small regions called constituencies, on the basis of population. Each constituency elects one person to the Lok Sabha and each elected member represents, as far as possible, the same number of people. For instance, though Kerala (38,863 sq km) is smaller than Arunachal Pradesh (83,743 sq km), in terms of area, it has more parliamentary constituencies than the latter. While Kerala has twenty seats, Arunachal Pradesh has only six seats. This is because the population of Kerala is more than that of Arunachal Pradesh.

The Lok Sabha continues for a period of five years from the date appointed for its first meeting but may be dissolved by the President before the end of the term. However, while a proclamation of Emergency is in operation, this period may be extended by Parliament by law for a maximum of one year at a time, but not exceeding beyond a period of six months after the proclamation has ceased to operate.

GOOD TO KNOW
- The Twelfth Lok Sabha had the shortest life span, lasting for around thirteen months, from 10 March 1998 to 26 April 1999.
- In the Lok Sabha, the Budget Session is the longest of the three sessions.
- Many illustrious people from different fields have been elected members of the Lok Sabha. In the 1984 General Elections, superstar Amitabh Bachchan defeated H. N. Bahuguna from the Allahabad seat and became a Lok Sabha member. Rajyavardhan Singh Rathore, who won a silver medal in shooting category at the 2004 Summer Olympics, was elected to the Lok Sabha in 2014. The late actor Sunil Dutt was elected to the Lok Sabha five times from the Mumbai North-West constituency. The famous physicist, Meghnad Saha, was also a member of the first Lok Sabha.

GLOSSARY

▸ Parliamentary Constituency: is a small region sending one member to the Lok Sabha. There are 543 parliamentary constituencies in India now, each electing one member to the Lok Sabha.

DISQUALIFICATION OF MEMBERSHIP FROM THE PARLIAMENT

A candidate can be disqualified from being chosen as a member or, an existing member can lose his/her membership of either House of Parliament if:

1. he holds any office of profit under the Government of India or the government of any state (other than an office exempted by Parliament by law). A person is not considered to hold an office of profit if he/she is a minister in the Union or in a state.
2. a competent court has declared that the person is of unsound mind;
3. a person has not been discharged by a court on cases relating to insolvency (a condition in which a person does not have enough money to pay off debts);
4. he is not a citizen of India or has voluntarily acquired citizenship of a foreign country;
5. he is disqualified by or under any law made by Parliament.

If any question arises as to whether a member of either House of Parliament has become subject to any of the above disqualifications, the President's decision, after consultation with the Election Commission, shall be final. The President, in consultation with the Election Commission, takes the final decision on whether a particular member of either House of Parliament has become subject to any of the above disqualifications.

PRESIDING OFFICERS OF THE LOK SABHA: THE SPEAKER AND THE DEPUTY SPEAKER

The Speaker and the Deputy Speaker are the Presiding Officers of the Lok Sabha. They are chosen from amongst the members in the first few sittings of the House. The Speaker holds office from the date of his/her election till the first sitting of the next Lok Sabha.

The Speaker is responsible for conducting business in the Lok Sabha. His functions include deciding whether a question is admissible or not; regulating discussions in the House, and deciding which member shall speak and for how long. The Speaker also certifies Money Bills and presides over joint sittings called in cases of disagreement between the two Houses on a legislative issue.

Although a member of the Lok Sabha, the Speaker does not vote in the House except in case of a tie. The Deputy Speaker performs the duties of the Speaker in his/her absence from the sitting of the House. However, in the absence of both the Speaker and Deputy Speaker, a member from the Panel of Chairmen presides over the House. When the offices of both the Speaker and Deputy Speaker become vacant, the duties of the office of the Speaker are performed by a member chosen by the President.

GOOD TO KNOW
- The Speaker of the Lok Sabha can only cast a vote in the House if there is a tie at the end of a decision. Till the Fifteenth Lok Sabha, no Speaker has had the opportunity to use this special power.
- Till date, Balram Jakhar has been the longest-serving Speaker of the Lok Sabha.

- M. A. Ayyangar was the first Deputy Speaker of the Lok Sabha.
- Jawaharlal Nehru referred to G. V. Mavalankar, the first Speaker of the Lok Sabha, as the 'Father of the Lok Sabha'.
- In the Lok Sabha, the words *Dharma Chakra Pravartnaya* are inscribed in Sanskrit on a wooden panel just above the Speaker's Chair. It means the setting the Wheel of Law in motion.

GLOSSARY

▶ Panel of Chairmen: consists of ten members of the House of the People who are nominated by the Speaker to preside over the House.

SPEAKERS OF THE LOK SABHA

1. G.V. Mavalankar — 15 May 1952–27 February 1956
2. M. A. Ayyangar — 8 March 1956–16 April 1962
3. Sardar Hukam Singh — 17 April 1962–16 March 1967
4. N. Sanjiva Reddy — 17 March 1967–19 July 1969
5. G.S. Dhillon — 8 August 1969–1 December 1975
6. Bali Ram Bhagat — 15 January 1976–25 March 1977
7. N. Sanjiva Reddy — 26 March 1977–13 July 1977
8. K.S. Hegde — 21 July 1977–21 January 1980
9. Balram Jakhar — 22 January 1980–18 December 1989
10. Rabi Ray — 19 December 1989–9 July 1991
11. Shivraj Patil — 10 July 1991–22 May 1996
12. P.A. Sangma — 25 May 1996–23 March 1998
13. G.M.C. Balayogi — 24 March 1998–3 March 2002
14. Manohar Joshi — 10 May 2002–2 June 2004
15. Somnath Chatterjee — 4 June 2004–31 May 2009
16. Meira Kumar — 4 June 2009–4 June 2014
17. Sumitra Mahajan — 6 June 2014–till date

THE LEADER OF THE HOUSE AND THE LEADER OF THE OPPOSITION IN THE LOK SABHA

The Leader of the House in the Lok Sabha refers to the Prime Minister, if he is a member of the House. If he is not, it refers to a minister who belongs to the House and is nominated/appointed by the Prime Minister to function as the Leader of the House. The Leader of the House plays an important role in the functioning of the Lok Sabha. He directly influences the course of business in the House. He is entrusted with the task of drawing up the programme of official business in the Lok Sabha, like Bills, motions and discussions on general or specific subjects. He decides which amendments are acceptable and which Private Members' Bills are to receive support of the government.

The Leader of the Opposition is a member of that party in Opposition to the government that has the maximum strength in terms of number (at least one-tenth of the strength of the House) and is recognised as such, by the Speaker of the Lok Sabha. The main responsibility of the Leader of the Opposition is to provide healthy criticism to the government and suggest alternative proposals and policies.

GOOD TO KNOW
- Jawaharlal Nehru, his daughter Indira Gandhi and his grandson Rajiv Gandhi, have all served as the Leader of the House in the Lok Sabha at different points in time.
- The minimum percentage of seats a political party has to win so that it can nominate a Leader of the Opposition is 10 per cent.
- Sonia Gandhi was the first woman to hold the post of Leader of the Opposition in the Lok Sabha.

COUNCIL OF MINISTERS

The Council of Ministers is a decision-making body of the government consisting of a select group of members of Parliament who help and advise the President in discharging his duties. It is collectively responsible to the House of the People. It consists of three different categories at the Union level: *a*) Cabinet Ministers, *b*) Ministers of State and *c*) Deputy Ministers.

It is headed by the Prime Minister who is appointed by the President. The other ministers are appointed from either House of Parliament by the President, on the advice of the Prime Minister. The maximum strength of the Council, including the Prime Minister, must not be more than 15 per cent of the total number of members of the House of the People.

GOOD TO KNOW
- A few of the important cabinet portfolios are Home Affairs, Finance, Defence, External Affairs, Railways, and Health and Family Welfare.
- A minister may also be appointed from outside Parliament, but he needs to get himself/herself elected to either House of Parliament within six months of entering office.
- Indira Gandhi is the only woman to have served as the Finance Minister of India.
- Shyama Prasad Mukherjee was the first person to resign from the Union Cabinet.

GLOSSARY
▶ Minister: refers to a member of the Council of Ministers.
▶ Ministers of State: are members of the Council of Ministers but not members of the Cabinet, and they can attend Cabinet meetings only when invited.

> **PEOPLE IN SPECIAL CAPACITIES ACCORDED CABINET RANKING**
>
> Nandan Nilekani, the co-founder of Infosys Ltd., was appointed as the Chairman of the Unique Identification Authority of India, an organisation set up to provide Aadhar cards carrying a 12-digit individual identification number to the people of India on behalf of the Government of India. As Chairman of the organisation, he was given a Cabinet rank. Before becoming the President of India, A. P. J. Kalam served as the Principal Scientific Advisor to the Government of India, in the rank of a Cabinet Minister. He was entrusted with the responsibility of formulating policies and developing strategies and missions.

THE PRIME MINISTER OF INDIA

The Leader of the party or coalition (group of parties) in majority becomes the Prime Minister of India.

The normal tenure of the Prime Minister of India as head of the Council of Ministers is five years. The minimum age at which a person can become the Prime Minister of India is twenty-five years.

As the Prime Minister is the head of the Union Council of Ministers, other ministers can only be appointed by the President on his recommendation. He has the power to allocate and reshuffle portfolios among the ministers. The Prime Minister presides over the meetings of the Council of Ministers and plays an important role in decision-making. He guides and coordinates the activities of all the ministers in the council of ministers. As he is the head of the Union Council of Ministers, his resignation or death automatically dissolves the Council.

The Prime Minister acts as the principal channel of communication between the President and Council of Ministers.

All the decisions of the Council regarding the affairs of administration of the Union and proposals for legislation are communicated to the President by the Prime Minister.

He advises the President with regard to the appointment of important officials like the Attorney General of India, Comptroller and Auditor General of India, Chairman and Members of the UPSC, Election Commissioners, Chairmen and Members of the Finance Commission, and so on.

The Prime Minister is the Chairman of the National Water Resources Council. He is also in direct charge of the Department of Atomic Energy and Department of Space. B. R. Ambedkar once likened the role of the US President with the Prime Minister and not the President of the Union.

> **GOOD TO KNOW**
> - The Prime Minister's Office (PMO) is headquartered in the South Block of the Secretariat Building, located on the Raisina Hill in New Delhi, flanking the Rashtrapati Bhavan.
> - Indira Gandhi was the only woman Prime Minister of India.
> - The Prime Minister can be a member of either House of Parliament.
> - Traditionally, the official residence of the Prime Minister of India is located on the Race Course Road in New Delhi.

SHORT BIOGRAPHIES OF PRIME MINISTERS OF INDIA

The position of the Prime Minister of India is an important one. He plays a crucial role in running the affairs of the country. Although India has been independent for more than sixty years, few Indians have had the opportunity to hold this esteemed position. Here is a short introduction to the Prime Ministers of India (in chronological order):

JAWAHARLAL NEHRU (15 August 1947–27 May 1964)*

Born in Allahabad, Uttar Pradesh, on 14 November 1889, Jawaharlal Nehru was educated at Harrow and Trinity College, Cambridge and the Inner Temple.

Nehru played a major role during the freedom struggle and became the first Prime Minister of independent India. He is chiefly remembered for laying down the foundations of the newly independent country by setting up organisations like the Planning Commission and the National Science Laboratories and nurturing institutions like the Parliament, a multi-party system and an independent judiciary. One of the key goals on his agenda for India was rapid industrialisation.

In world politics, Nehru proposed the policy of non-alignment and the principle of Panchsheel (the five principles of peaceful coexistence).

Nehru was awarded the Bharat Ratna in 1955. He passed away on 27 May 1964.

GULZARI LAL NANDA (27 May 1964–9 June 1964)

Gulzari Lal Nanda was born on 4 July 1898 in Sialkot (now in Pakistan). He was educated in Lahore, Agra and Allahabad and, in 1921, became Professor of Economics at the National College (Bombay).

Inspired by the principles of Mahatma Gandhi, Gulzari Lal Nanda actively participated in the freedom struggle and later helped draw up the First Five Year Plan. He served as the interim Prime Minister of India on two occasions: after Jawaharlal Nehru's death (1964) and after Lal Bahadur Shastri's demise (1966). He was an expert in handling labour issues and played an important part in organising the Indian National Trade

---

*The dates within brackets denote the tenure of each Prime Minister.

Union. He had an active political life and headed important ministries till the 1960s.

Gulzari Lal Nanda was awarded the Bharat Ratna in 1997. He passed away on 15 January 1998.

LAL BAHADUR SHASTRI (9 June 1964–11 January 1966)

Born on 2 October 1904 in Mughalsarai, Uttar Pradesh, Lal Bahadur Shastri was educated at the Kashi Vidya Peeth in Varanasi.

Shastri joined the freedom struggle, in response to Gandhiji's call for non-cooperation. After India became independent, he held many important ministries like Railways and Transport, Commerce and Industry and Home Affairs.

In 1965, as Prime Minister, Shastri successfully led the country during the war with Pakistan (1965). He raised the slogan of 'Jai Jawan, Jai Kisan' to acknowledge the role of soldiers and farmers in nation-building. In 1966, he signed the historic peace treaty with President Ayub Khan of Pakistan in Tashkent (present-day Uzbekistan) after the war.

Shastri died in Tashkent in 1966, shortly after signing the peace treaty. He was conferred the Bharat Ratna posthumously in 1966.

GULZARI LAL NANDA (11 January 1966–24 January 1966)

See page 92.

INDIRA GANDHI (24 January 1966–24 March 1977)

Born on 19 November 1917 to Pandit Jawaharlal Nehru and Kamala Nehru, Indira Gandhi was educated in a number of places including Shantiniketan and Oxford.

Hailing from an illustrious political family, Indira Gandhi was involved in the freedom struggle from an early age. She served as the Minister for Information and Broadcasting before becoming the first woman Prime Minister of India in 1966. Some of her major achievements include the nationalisation of banks, the first nuclear tests in Pokhran and the birth of Bangladesh. She also raised the slogan 'Garibi Hatao'.

Indira Gandhi died on 31 October 1984 in New Delhi. In India, her birth anniversary is observed as the National Integration Day. She was conferred the Bharat Ratna in 1971.

MORARJI DESAI (24 March 1977–28 July 1979)

Born on 29 February 1896 in Gujarat, Morarji Desai graduated from the Wilson Civil Service of the then Bombay Province in 1918 and served as a Deputy Collector for more than a decade.

Desai resigned from government service to actively participate in the struggle for independence. After India became independent, he became the Chief Minister of Bombay in 1952. He held many important cabinet portfolios before becoming the Deputy Prime Minister in 1967.

In 1977, Desai became the first non-Congress Prime Minister of India since independence, when he headed a coalition government formed by the Janata Party. As Prime Minister, he tried to strengthen India's relations with Pakistan and China. His government undid many of the amendments made to the Constitution during Emergency.

Desai passed away in 1995 at the ripe old age of 99. He was conferred the Bharat Ratna in 1991.

CHAUDHARY CHARAN SINGH (28 July 1979–14 January 1980)

Born on 23 December 1902 in Uttar Pradesh, Chaudhary Charan Singh completed his LL.B and became a civil lawyer in Ghaziabad. He held various important political positions in Uttar Pradesh before becoming the Prime Minister of India in

1979. Charan Singh was in office for 171 days but never faced Parliament as one of the supporting parties withdrew its support. He continued to function as caretaker Prime Minister till fresh elections were held.

Charan Singh had a keen interest in the lives of the farmers and addressed a number of issues relating to the community. He played a key role in formulating and implementing the Zamindari Abolition Act. He also authored books like *Abolition of Zamindari*, *Cooperative Farming X-rayed* and *India's Poverty and Its Solution*.

In recognition of Charan Singh's services to the farmers' community, his birth anniversary is also observed as Kisan Diwas.

INDIRA GANDHI (14 January 1980–31 October 1984)
See page 93.

RAJIV GANDHI (31 October 1984–2 December 1989)
Born on 20 August 1944 in Bombay to Indira and Feroze Gandhi, Rajiv Gandhi was a pilot by profession. He was their eldest son.

Rajiv Gandhi became the youngest Prime Minister of India when he assumed office at the age of forty, succeeding Indira Gandhi. As Prime Minister, he sought to improve productivity in industries through the use of modern technology. He launched the Ganga Action Plan to improve the quality of water and prevent pollution. The Anti-Defection law, came into force during Rajiv Gandhi's tenure. It sets the provisions for disqualification of elected members of Parliament or a State Legislature on the grounds of defection to another political party. He also sent the Indian Peace Keeping Force to Sri Lanka to restore peace.

Rajiv Gandhi died in 1991 and was conferred the Bharat Ratna posthumously that year. His birth anniversary is celebrated as Sadbhavana Diwas (Harmony Day).

V. P. SINGH (2 December 1989–10 November 1990)

Born on 25 June 1931 at Allahabad, Uttar Pradesh, V. P. Singh was educated at Varanasi and Pune. He actively participated in the Bhoodan Movement in 1957 and served as the Union Finance Minister in the mid-1980s.

V. P. Singh is remembered for his efforts to implement the recommendations of the Mandal Commission. He passed away in Delhi on 27 November 2008.

CHANDRA SHEKHAR (10 November 1990–21 June 1991)

Born on 1 July 1927 in Uttar Pradesh, Chandra Shekhar received his master's degree in Political Science from Allahabad University.

During his years in the Congress, Chandra Shekhar came to be known as a 'Young Turk' for his conviction, courage and integrity. In 1977, he became President of the Janata Party. In the early 1980s, he undertook a *padayatra* of 4,620 km from Kanyakumari to Rajghat in Delhi to establish a rapport with the masses. Chandra Shekhar had to resign a few months after becoming the Prime Minister as the Congress (I) Party withdrew its support.

Chandra Shekhar passed away at the age of eighty in 2007.

P. V. NARASIMHA RAO (21 June 1991–16 May 1996)

Born on 28 June 1921, at Karimnagar in present-day Telangana, P.V. Narasimha Rao studied at Osmania University in Hyderabad and at the Bombay and Nagpur universities, eventually receiving a law degree.

During his tenure as the Prime Minister, Rao launched the economic liberalisation programme. A significant part of the public sector was privatised, the licence raj was abolished to promote more competition in the market and policies on foreign investments were modified to allow for more investments.

P. V. Narasimha Rao passed away in 2004.

ATAL BIHARI VAJPAYEE (16 May 1996–1 June 1996)
See page 98.

H.D. DEVE GOWDA (1 June 1996–21 April 1997)
Born on 18 May 1933, in the village of Haradanahalli in Karnataka, H.D. Deve Gowda plunged into active politics at the early age of twenty, when he joined the Congress Party in 1953, just after receiving a diploma in civil engineering.

As Prime Minister heading the United Front coalition government, Gowda signed the important Ganges Water Sharing Treaty with Bangladesh. He continues to be active in politics and is a member of the Sixteenth Lok Sabha from Karnataka.

I. K. GUJRAL (21 April 1997–19 March 1998)
Born on 4 December 1919, in Jhelum (in the undivided Punjab, now in Pakistan), I.K. Gujral earned many degrees including M.A., B.Com., Ph.D. and D.Litt.

Gujral was the External Affairs Minister in Deve Gowda's government. In April 1997, Deve Gowda, the incumbent Prime Minister, lost a vote of confidence in the Lok Sabha. In his place, Gujral was elected the Prime Minister. However, when the government fell due to withdrawal of support, Gujral resigned and remained in a caretaker capacity until a new government was formed. Despite his brief tenure, he made his mark by introducing the Gujral Doctrine, a policy grounded on India's unilaterally reaching out diplomatically to its neighbours without the expectation of reciprocity.

Gujral tried to improve relations with India's neighbours, especially with Pakistan and Bangladesh. He passed away on 30 November 2012.

ATAL BIHARI VAJPAYEE (19 March 1998–22 May 2004)

Atal Bihari Vajpayee was born in Gwalior on 25 December 1924. Educated in Gwalior and Kanpur Vajpayee holds an M.A. (Political Science) degree. Vajpayee participated in the freedom struggle and went to jail in 1942. He was detained during the Emergency in 1975–77.

Vajpayee served as India's External Affairs Minister from 1977 to 1979. He was Leader of the Opposition during the term of the Eleventh Lok Sabha. Vajpayee was sworn in as the Prime Minister of India on three occasions in the years 1996, 1998 and 1999.

One of Vajpayee's most important initiatives during his term as Prime Minister heading the National Democratic Alliance (NDA) government was the Pokhran-II nuclear tests, boosting India's defence capabilities. He also launched two big projects: the National Highways Development Project (NHDP) and the Pradhan Mantri Gram Sadak Yojana (PMGSY) to link every village of the nation by road. In his effort to improve India's relationship with Pakistan, Vajpayee launched the Delhi–Lahore bus service. He also successfully led the nation during the Kargil War in 1999.

A prolific writer and a great orator, Vajpayee has many accomplishments to his credit. In 2014, he was named for India's highest civilian honour, the Bharat Ratna.

MANMOHAN SINGH (22 May 2004–26 May 2014)

A world-renowned economist, Manmohan Singh served as the Prime Minister of India for two successive terms. He was born on 26 September 1932, in Gah (in present-day Pakistan). An eminent economist, he held many important economic advisory posts with the government before becoming the Finance Minister in the Narasimha Rao government in 1991. Singh was responsible for a major turnaround in the Indian economy at the time.

In 2004, Singh succeeded Atal Bihari Vajpayee as the Prime Minister of India in the United Progressive Alliance (UPA) coalition. Some of the measures that came into force during Manmohan Singh's tenure as the Prime Minister were the VAT, NREGA and RTI. The Value Added Tax (VAT) was a concept, where taxes were levied on the amount of value addition done at each stage of transaction in commercial activities. The National Rural Employment Guarantee Act (NREGA) tried to enhance the security of livelihood in rural areas by providing at least 100 days of guaranteed employment in every financial year. The Right to Information (RTI) is an Act that empowers the citizens of India to gain access to information that is held by public authorities, thus ensuring transparency and accountability in the process.

NARENDRA DAMODARDAS MODI (26 May 2014–till date)

Narendra Damodardas Modi is the current Prime Minister of India. He is the first Prime Minister to be born after the independence of India. Born on 17 September 1950, in Vadnagar, Gujarat, he served as the Chief Minister of Gujarat before becoming the Prime Minister in 2014.

As the Prime Minister, Modi has launched various schemes including the Pradhan Mantri Jan Dhan Yojana (PMJDY), to ensure that every household in India has at least one bank account.

> **GOOD TO KNOW**
> - Jawaharlal Nehru holds the record for being the Prime Minister of India for the longest period, approximately seventeen years.
> - The Third Lok Sabha saw three full-time Prime Ministers

and one acting Prime Minister. Jawaharlal Nehru was elected Prime Minister in 1962. When he passed away in 1964, Gulzari Lal Nanda served as the acting Prime Minister till Lal Bahadur Shastri assumed office. Gulzari Lal Nanda again held the position after the death of Lal Bahadur Shastri in 1966. Indira Gandhi, who was elected Prime Minister by the Congress, took over the reins from Gulzari Lal Nanda after his second stint.
- The music album 'Samvedna', is a collection of poems written by Atal Bihari Vajpayee. It was composed and sung by the late ghazal singer Jagjit Singh.
- On 20 August 1991, the India Post issued what is said to be its single largest stamp then. The stamp featured Rajiv Gandhi.
- Atal Bihari Vajpayee appeared as himself in the 1977 film *Chala Murari Hero Banne*.
- As a child, Indira Gandhi founded the Bal Charkha Sangh and the Vanar Sena to help the Congress Party.
- Former Prime Minister Lal Bahadur Shastri shares his birth anniversary with Mahatma Gandhi.

GENERAL ELECTIONS

General Elections are normally held every five years in order to elect representatives to the Lok Sabha. For this purpose, the territory of India is divided into constituencies with each constituency electing and sending one member to the Lok Sabha. Any citizen of India who is above eighteen years of age, and is not disqualified by the Constitution or law, is eligible to vote. The Election Commission of India conducts and supervises the procedure for these elections. As many as sixteen General Elections to the Lok Sabha have been held till date.

ALLOCATION OF SEATS IN THE LOK SABHA

States
1. Andhra Pradesh— 25
2. Arunachal Pradesh—2
3. Assam—14
4. Bihar—40
5. Chhattisgarh—11
6. Goa—2
7. Gujarat—26
8. Haryana—10
9. Himachal Pradesh—4
10. Jammu and Kashmir—6
11. Jharkhand—14
12. Karnataka—28
13. Kerala—20
14. Madhya Pradesh—29
15. Maharashtra—48
16. Manipur—2
17. Meghalaya—2
18. Mizoram—1
19. Nagaland—1
20. Odisha—21
21. Punjab—13
22. Rajasthan—25
23. Sikkim—1
24. Tamil Nadu—39
25. Telangana—17
26. Tripura—2
27. Uttar Pradesh—80
28. Uttarakhand—5
29. West Bengal—42

Contd.

Union Territories
1. Andaman and Nicobar Islands—1
2. Chandigarh—1
3. Dadra and Nagar Haveli—1
4. Daman and Diu—1
5. National Capital Territory of Delhi—7
6. Lakshadweep—1
7. Puducherry—1

LOK SABHA ELECTIONS IN INDIA

Introduction

Purpose
1. To elect members to the House of the People (Lok Sabha).
2. To identify a party or coalition that will form the government at the Centre.

Frequency
1. Every five years, or
2. Called earlier by the President if the Lok Sabha is dissolved in term. This can happen if the government loses confidence of the majority of members and if there is no alternative government to take over.

Key Players

Election Commission Of India
1. Independent constitutional authority entrusted with holding regular, free and fair elections.
2. Headquartered at New Delhi.

Contd.

Political Parties
1. Should be registered with the Election Commission of India.
2. They should follow the Model Code of Conduct issued by the Election Commission of India to ensure fair elections.

Voters
1. Any Indian citizen who is at least eighteen years of age on 1 January of the year, who ordinarily lives in the constituency concerned and is not disqualified by the Constitution or law.
2. Eligible elector has to be registered in the respective constituency.
3. Indian citizens living abroad also can be enrolled at the address given in their passports.

Candidates
1. Any Indian citizen over the age of twenty-five, who is also registered as a voter.
2. Any member of a political party or an independent candidate.
3. General candidates should be able to deposit ₹25,000 and the SC and ST candidates should be able to deposit, ₹12,500. They also need to file affidavit about their assets, liabilities, criminal background and educational qualifications.
4. The candidate has to have all the other qualifications that may be prescribed by Parliament by law.

Contd.

The Electoral Process

What Are Parliamentary Constituencies?
1. The territory of India is divided into 543 constituencies.
2. Each one is based on the number of seats allocated to each state and union territory, on the basis of their population.
3. The size is determined by Delimitation Commission of India.
4. One member is elected to the Lok Sabha from each constituency, filling 543 of 545 seats.
5. At most, two members are nominated by the President from the Anglo-Indian community.

How Does The Electoral Process Work?
1. Each elector can vote for one candidate.
2. The candidate with maximum votes wins.

How Are The Elections Scheduled?
1. The elections are executed by the Election Commission of India.
2. Weather, festivals, school exams, etc. are considered.
3. Maximum electoral participation is sought.
4. Generally elections are held in phases to ensure effective security arrangements for a peaceful poll.

What Are Manifestos And Election Symbols?
1. Manifestos are issued by parties and candidates on the eve of an election, which contain details of what they wish to implement if elected, outlining their strengths and pointing out the failures of opponents.
2. Election symbols are allotted to recognised parties and independent candidates to enable illiterate voters to identify the party and candidate they wish to vote for.

Contd.

Electoral Participation

Electoral Rolls
1. Electoral rolls are annually updated lists of registered electors in each constituency.

EPIC
1. The Electors' Photo Identity Card is provided to each individual elector upon registration.

SVEEP
1. It is an acronym for Systematic Voter Education and Electoral Participation.
2. It aims to improve electoral participation and build up a culture of participative democracy.

Regulatory Mechanisms

Supervising Elections
1. Executed by Observers appointed by the ECI
   In order to.
   i. promote fair conduct of campaigns.
   ii. promote free and ethical voting.
   iii. monitor election expenditure.
2. Types of Observers
   a. General Observers.
   b. Police Observers.
   c. Expenditure Observers.
   d. Awareness Observers.
   e. Micro Observers.

Model Code Of Conduct
1. For political parties and contestants.

Contd.

2. Broad guidelines on conduct during the campaign evolved by the ECI on the basis of consensus among political parties.
3. To maintain campaigns on healthy lines and to ensure a level playing field.

Limit On Poll Expenses
1. Tight legal limits on poll expenditure by candidates

Polling Management

Electronic Voting Machines
1. Voting by secret ballot.

Polling Stations
1. Usually set up in public institutions.
2. Within 2 km of every voter.
3. No polling station to deal with more than 1,500 voters.

Postal Ballot
1. Certain sections of voters are entitled to vote by post like the members of the armed forces.

Proxy Voting
1. Option to vote through the postal ballot is available to service voters belonging to the Armed Forces or to members belonging to a force to which the Army Act applies.

Indelible Ink
1. Applied to a voter's left fore-finger before permitting him/her to vote.
2. Used to control fake voting.

Contd.

3. Dries up in sixty seconds and usually remains for a few months.
4. Cannot be removed by chemicals, detergents or oil.

Counting of Votes
1. Done after completion of all phases of polling.
2. Under the supervision of Returning Officers and Election Observers.
3. Counting for all 543 constituencies done on a single day.
4. Results declared within a few hours.

THE SIXTEENTH LOK SABHA ELECTIONS—INTERESTING FACTS

- According to the Election Commission of India reports released on 14 February 2014, there were a total of 81,45,91,184 registered electors in the country. Out of the total, the states together accounted for 98.27 per cent of electors. Uttar Pradesh, with more than 13.43 crore electors, had the largest number of electors, while Sikkim with around 3.62 lakh electors had the smallest number of electors, among the states. Of the total number of registered voters, there were 2,31,61,296 electors aged between eighteen and nineteen years, thus constituting 2.8 per cent of the national electorate.
- The total number of political parties that participated in the Sixteenth General Elections was 464. This comprised six national parties, thirty-nine state parties and 419 unrecognised parties.
- Malkajgiri in Andhra Pradesh with 29,53,915 electors had the largest number of electors while Lakshadweep with 47,972 electors had the smallest number of electors.

Contd.

- The Sixteenth Lok Sabha has sixty-one women members, the highest till date. In the 2014 Elections, 8,251 candidates contested the elections, out of which only 668 were women.
- The 2014 General Elections saw the highest ever voter turnout in India with 66.4 per cent of the electorate casting votes.
- Narendra Modi is the first Prime Minister to have contested from two different constituencies and won from both. The constituencies were Varanasi and Vadodara.
- No single party in the Sixteenth Lok Sabha had the requisite number of seats to qualify as the Principal Opposition Party. A party needs to have at least fifty-four seats, which is one-tenth of the current Lok Sabha strength, to qualify as the Principal Opposition Party.
- Of the total members of the Sixteenth Lok Sabha, around 53 per cent are under the age of fifty-five years.
- At twenty-six years of age, Dushyant Chautala and Heena Gavit are the youngest Lok Sabha MPs in the Sixteenth Lok Sabha, while L.K. Advani, at eighty-six, is the oldest.
- For the first time in General Elections in India, 'None of the Above' (NOTA) was an option on the Electronic Voting Machine (EVM), whereby a voter could press this button if he/she did not wish to vote for any of the candidates.

GOOD TO KNOW
- The total amount spent on the First General Elections is said to be around ₹10.45 crore.
- The indelible ink used in General Elections is manufactured by Mysore Paints and Varnish Limited (MPVL), a company based in Mysore, Karnataka.
- While a serving President of India can vote in a General

Election, most have chosen not to do so to maintain their neutrality.
- An Electronic Voting Machine consists of two Units—a Control Unit and a Balloting Unit.
- In India, the term 'delimitation' means the act of fixing the limits or boundaries of territorial constituencies in a province that has a legislative body.

THE RAJYA SABHA

HISTORY, COMPOSITION AND TERM

The Rajya Sabha is the Upper House of Parliament. The Constituent Assembly had debated the need for a Second Chamber in independent India and decided that India, with its size and diversity, needed a Parliament with two chambers. Thus, the second chamber known as the 'Council of States', came into being. It was first constituted in April 1952. The name 'Rajya Sabha' was given to the Council of States in 1954.

The Rajya Sabha is composed of not more than 250 members out of whom 238 represent states and union territories while twelve are nominated by the President of India.

The Rajya Sabha is a permanent body. It cannot be dissolved; nearly one-third of its members retire at the end of every second year. Normally, the term of a member of Rajya Sabha is six years. But if a member resigns, dies or is disqualified before the end of his term, a 'bye-election' is held to fill in the seat. The member filling in for someone will only serve for the remaining period of the term.

Unlike the Lok Sabha where members are elected through direct elections, the members of the Rajya Sabha are elected by the method of indirect election.

The representatives of each state are elected by the elected members of the Legislative Assembly of that state. Only two union territories, Delhi and Puducherry, are represented in the

Rajya Sabha. The representatives of these union territories are elected by the members of their respective Electoral Colleges.

The twelve members, nominated by the President, are people with special knowledge or practical experience in the fields of literature, science, art and social service.

A citizen of India who is at least thirty years of age and has all other qualifications that are prescribed by Parliament by law is eligible to be a member of the Rajya Sabha.

The Rajya Sabha has the special power to:

1. make laws related to matters mentioned in the State List, in the interest of the country;
2. create All India Services;
3. approve Proclamations if the Lok Sabha stands dissolved or dissolves before the approval.

ALLOCATION OF SEATS IN THE RAJYA SABHA

States and Union Territories
1. Andhra Pradesh—11
2. Arunachal Pradesh—1
3. Assam–7
4. Bihar —16
5. Chhattisgarh—5
6. Goa–1
7. Gujarat—11
8. Haryana—5
9. Himachal Pradesh—3
10. Jammu and Kashmir—4
11. Jharkhand—6
12. Karnataka—12
13. Kerala—9

Contd.

14. Madhya Pradesh—11
15. Maharashtra—19
16. Manipur—1
17. Meghalaya—1
18. Mizoram—1
19. Nagaland—1
20. National Capital Territory of Delhi—3
21. Odisha—10
22. Puducherry—1
23. Punjab—7
24. Rajasthan—10
25. Sikkim—1
26. Tamil Nadu–18
27. Telangana—7
28. Tripura—1
29. Uttarakhand—3
30. Uttar Pradesh—31
31. West Bengal—16

GOOD TO KNOW
- In the Rajya Sabha, the election held every second year to elect new members to replace those retiring, is called a 'Biennial Election'.
- There are four methods of voting in the Rajya Sabha: Voice vote, Counting, Division by automatic vote recorders and Division by going into the Lobbies.
- The nominated members of Rajya Sabha are not entitled to vote in the election of the President of India.
- One of India's greatest cricketers, Sachin Tendulkar, is a member of the Rajya Sabha.
- As of 2014, Najma Heptulla is the longest-serving member in the Rajya Sabha.

- Rukmini Devi Arundale was the first woman to be nominated to the Rajya Sabha.

PRESIDING OFFICERS OF THE RAJYA SABHA: THE CHAIRMAN AND THE DEPUTY CHAIRMAN

The Chairman and the Deputy Chairman are the Presiding Officers of the Rajya Sabha and are responsible for carrying out the proceedings of the House. While the Vice President of India is the ex-officio Chairman of the Rajya Sabha, the Deputy Chairman is chosen from amongst its members. Besides the Chairman and the Deputy Chairman, there is a Panel of Vice Chairmen nominated by the Chairman of the Rajya Sabha. A member of this panel handles the proceedings of the House in the absence of the Chairman and Deputy Chairman.

GOOD TO KNOW
- S. Radhakrishnan was the first Vice President and ex-officio Chairman of the Rajya Sabha to become the President of India.
- Krishan Kant was the first Vice President and the ex-officio Chairman of the Rajya Sabha to die in office.

THE LEADER OF THE HOUSE AND THE LEADER OF THE OPPOSITION IN THE RAJYA SABHA

The Leader of the House plays an important part in the smooth functioning of the business in the Rajya Sabha. The Leader of the House in Rajya Sabha is normally the Prime Minister, if he is its member. If he is not a member, he nominates a minister belonging to the House, to hold the position. It is the responsibility of the Leader of the House to ensure a healthy environment in the House. To this end, he maintains a cordial relationship with all the sections of the House including the members of the Opposition, individual ministers and the Presiding Officer.

A member of the Rajya Sabha, who is the leader of the largest party opposing the government, having at least 10 percent of the total strength of the House, is recognised as the Leader of the Opposition in the Rajya Sabha by the Chairman. The role of the Leader of the Opposition is to criticise constructively, find fault and present alternative proposals/policies, etc.

> **GOOD TO KNOW**
> - Shyam Nandan Mishra was the first Leader of the Opposition in the Rajya Sabha.

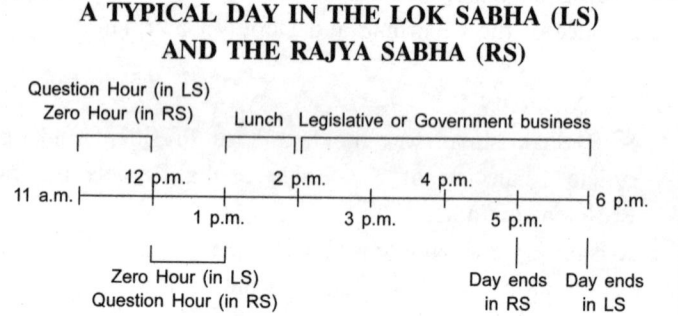

A typical day for a parliamentarian begins at 11 a.m. and ends at 6 p.m. in the Lok Sabha and 5 p.m. in the Rajya Sabha. Although there is a provision for an hour-long lunch break from 1 p.m. to 2 p.m., the MPs may continue working through the break and beyond 5 p.m. and 6 p.m. respectively if they feel the need to do so. While the Parliament is in session, it does not normally sit on weekends and some other holidays.

In the Lok Sabha, a normal day begins with the Question Hour and is followed by the Zero Hour. In the Rajya Sabha, there has been a reversal of the order. Here, the day begins

Contd.

with the Zero Hour and is followed by the Question Hour. After lunch, listed business is taken up in the House. It involves discussions on important Bills, the Budget and other issues of national importance.

Question Hour

Normally, the first hour of a sitting of Lok Sabha and till recently, the Rajya Sabha, is devoted to asking and responding to Questions. In Parliamentary parlance, it is referred to as the Question Hour. It is one of the most significant proceedings in Parliament. It is important because the members can obtain information directly from ministers on matters related to governance. Through this device, the members question the functioning of the government, report grievances of the people and expose the lapses of the authorities concerned. This leads to more accountability on part of the government. Through the Question Hour the government is able to quickly feel the pulse of the nation and adapt its policies and actions accordingly.

Zero Hour

Although it is not formally recognised in the parliamentary procedure in India, the Zero Hour traditionally refers to the time before any listed business is taken up in the House. It starts around 12 p.m. in the Lok Sabha and 11 a.m. in the Rajya Sabha. While it is preceded by the Question Hour in the Lok Sabha, it is followed by the Question Hour in the Rajya Sabha.

RULES OF PROCEDURE

In order to ensure the proper functioning of Parliament, each House has been provided with a set of rules compiled

Contd.

as Rules of Procedure. These rules regulate the functioning of the members and the proceedings of each House. The Speaker of the Lok Sabha and the Chairman of the Rajya Sabha are guided by the Rules of Procedure in overseeing the function of their respective Houses.

SECRETARIATS

Each House of Parliament has a separate secretarial staff. The Rajya Sabha Secretariat functions under the guidance and control of the Chairman, Rajya Sabha and the Lok Sabha Secretariat does so under the guidance of the Speaker of the Lok Sabha. The Lok Sabha Secretariat and the Rajya Sabha Secretariat are responsible for coordinating the functioning of the respective Houses. Both Lok Sabha and Rajya Sabha Secretariats are headed by their respective Secretary-Generals.

UNION BUDGET AND BILLS

UNION BUDGET

The estimated income and expenditure of the government for the forthcoming financial year is laid out before Parliament, usually in the month of February and it is known as the Union Budget or the Annual Financial Statement. Two types of budgets are presented in the Lok Sabha, namely, the General Budget and the Railway Budget. The General Budget is presented by the Union Minister of Finance and the Railway Budget by the Union Minister of Railways.

GOOD TO KNOW
- The first time the Budget papers were prepared in Hindi was in 1955–56.
- The word Budget comes from the French word *bougette*, meaning 'leather bag' for documents or money.
- The Finance Minister of India, on the day of the Budget, is often seen holding a briefcase aloft for photographers. The custom is inspired by the British Parliament where the Chancellor of the Exchequer generally carries the Budget statement to the House of Commons in the famous red leather briefcase.
- P. Chidambaram, a former Finance Minister, always ended his Budget speech by quoting from the works of the great Tamil poet Thiruvalluvar.

- The Union Budget of India is usually presented on the last working day of February.
- R. K. Shanmukham Chetty presented the first Union Budget of independent India.
- Until the year 2000 the annual Budget in India was presented at 5 p.m. This practice was inherited from the Colonial Era.

GLOSSARY

▸ Financial Year (of India): starts on 1 April of a year and ends on 31 March in the following year.

BILLS

A Bill is the draft of a legislative proposal. It becomes an Act after it is passed by both Houses of Parliament and signed by the President.

A Bill, other than money and financial Bills, may be introduced in either House of the Parliament. If it is introduced by a minister, it is called a Government Bill but if it is introduced by a Private Member, it is known as a Private Members' Bill. (Most members of Parliament are not ministers and they are referred to as Private Members.) Depending on their contents, Bills may be classified into the following divisions:

1. Original Bills (Bills containing new proposals, ideas or policies);
2. Amending Bills (Bills that modify, amend or revise the existing Acts);
3. Consolidating Bills (Bills that dwell upon consolidating existing laws on a particular subject);
4. Expiring Laws (Continuance) Bills (Bills to continue an expiring Act);
5. Repealing Bills (Bills seeking to revoke existing Acts);
6. Bills to replace Ordinances;

7. Constitution (Amendment) Bills;
8. Money and Financial Bills.

A Bill is regarded as a 'Money Bill' if it contains only provisions related to the following matters:

1. taxes;
2. financial issues related to the Government of India;
3. the management of funds from the Consolidated Fund or the Contingency Fund of India, etc.

A Money Bill can be introduced only in the Lok Sabha. The Speaker of the Lok Sabha has the sole power of deciding whether a Bill is a Money Bill. The members of the Rajya Sabha cannot make amendments in a Money Bill passed by the Lok Sabha although they may recommend changes in the Bill. The Lok Sabha may accept or reject any or all of the recommendations of the Rajya Sabha. If a Money Bill passed by the Lok Sabha is sent to the Rajya Sabha, it must be returned to the Lok Sabha within fourteen days of its receipt, otherwise it will be considered to have been passed by both Houses. When the Bill has been passed by the Houses of Parliament, it is sent to the President for his assent.

GOOD TO KNOW
- An average of seventy-two Bills a year was passed in the first Lok Sabha. A record 118 Bills were passed by Parliament in 1976.

PROCEDURAL DEVICES USED IN PARLIAMENT

During the sitting of the Lok Sabha and the Rajya Sabha, the MPs use various devices which are essentially tools or methods for raising and discussing issues related to legislative work. Some of these are:

Contd.

Calling Attention: When a member of either House, with prior permission of the Speaker in case of the Lok Sabha and the Chairman in case of the Rajya Sabha, addresses a Question to a minister on an issue of urgent public importance and the minister gives an answer or asks for time to reply, it is called 'Calling Attention'.

Half-an-Hour Discussion: If a member in the Lok Sabha feels that the answer given to a Starred or Unstarred or Short Notice Question is not complete and needs to be explained further, he may ask the Speaker to let him raise a Discussion in the House for half an hour. In the Rajya Sabha, the Chairman similarly allots half-an-hour on any day of the week for raising a matter of public importance for Discussion, typically, on a subject which has been discussed recently, but needs further clarification.

Motion: Any formal proposal made by a member of the House in order to obtain a decision of the House is called a 'Motion'.

Adjournment Motion: This Motion calls for the postponement of the regular business of the House in order to discuss an issue of public importance requiring immediate attention. This device cannot be used in the Rajya Sabha.

Motion of No-Confidence: The Council of Ministers is responsible to the House of the People. If the House expresses a lack of confidence in the Council of Ministers, it may pass a Motion of No-Confidence to remove the ministry. The Council, in that case, has to win the confidence of the House by moving a Motion of Confidence.

No-Day-Yet-Named-Motion: If the Speaker of the Lok Sabha admits Notice of a Motion, forwards it to the minister concerned without a date being fixed for its discussion, it

Contd.

is called a 'No-Day-Yet-Named Motion'. In case of Rajya Sabha, it is the Chairman who admits Notice of a Motion.

Parliamentary Questions: An important device that empowers members of Parliament to elicit factual information from the government on a matter of public interest is Parliamentary Questions. These questions are categorised as Starred, Unstarred and Short Notice Questions.

1. **Starred Questions**: These are questions that need oral answers during the Question Hour, on the floor of the House. They are called Starred Questions because they carry a distinguishing asterisk mark. Around twenty such questions are listed every day.
2. **Unstarred Questions**: These are questions to which written answers are given by ministers. Up to 155 such questions are listed each day in a separate list in the Rajya Sabha. In the Lok Sabha, generally around 230 such questions can be listed on a day.
3. **Short Notice Questions**: These questions are normally asked at a notice shorter than that prescribed for Starred and Unstarred Questions. These must relate to a subject matter considered to be of urgent public importance by the Chairman in the Rajya Sabha and the Speaker in the Lok Sabha.

Resolution: The views and decisions of a House are declared in the form of resolutions. When a House agrees on a question, it acquires the form of either a resolution or an order. Resolutions may be categorised as *a*) Private Members' Resolutions (which are moved by a member, not

Contd.

a minister); *b*) Government Resolutions (which are moved by ministers); *c*) Statutory Resolutions (which are moved keeping in mind a provision contained in the Constitution or an Act of Parliament).

Special Mention: If a member of the Lok Sabha wants to raise a matter of public importance (which is not a Point of Order or which cannot be raised under any other rule), he/she can do so through a Special Mention. It is a device that allows one to express oneself in not more than 150 words, after giving prior notice. In the Rajya Sabha, a member is allowed to make a Special Mention through a text not exceeding 250 words, by giving prior notice.

TERMS USED IN PARLIAMENT

Some of the terms used during the course of Parliamentary activity are:

Adjournment of the House: When the sitting or proceedings of the House is postponed from one specified time to another, it is called Adjournment. When no definite date is fixed for its next sitting, it is called Adjournment *sine die*. The Latin phrase *sine die* means 'without a day'.

Dissolution: It means the end of the life of the Lok Sabha either by an order made by the President or on the expiration of the period of five years from the date appointed for its first meeting.

Ordinance: Article 123 of the Constitution empowers the President of India to make laws through Ordinances when Parliamentary enactment on the subject is not possible.

Prorogation: When the Session of the House is brought to end by the President's order, it is termed as a Prorogation. It applies both to the Lok Sabha and the Rajya Sabha.

Contd.

> **Quorum**: The minimum number of members that need to be present at a Sitting of the House, or a committee to make the proceedings of that Sitting officially acceptable. The Quorum for a sitting of either House is one-tenth of the total number of members of that House.
>
> **Roll of Members**: Before taking their seats for the first time in the House, the newly elected members need to sign this register.
>
> **Sitting of the House**: A Sitting of the House is constituted when it is presided over by the Presiding Officer or a member appointed/nominated to preside over a Sitting of the House.
>
> **Summons**: An official communication issued to the members of the House informing them of the place, date and time of the commencement of a Session.
>
> **Whip**: A member of Parliament from a political party who has been entrusted with the task of managing the affairs of his/her party inside Parliament is called a Whip.

Many committees are formed in the Parliament for various purposes. Here are the details:

> ### PARLIAMENTARY COMMITTEES
>
> Parliamentary Committees are formed to assist the Legislature in handling a wide variety and large volume of work. These may be categorised as Ad hoc Committees and Standing Committees.
>
> Ad Hoc Committees are temporary committees that cease to exist once they finish their work and submit a report on the specific task assigned to them. Examples include committees for specific Bills. The Railway Convention Committee and Committees on the Draft Five Year Plans are some of the others.

Contd.

> Standing Committees are permanent committees whose members are either elected or nominated every year, or from time to time. The work of these committees is of continuous nature. Examples include Business Advisory Committee, Committee of Privileges, and Committee on Petitions and Rules Committee.
>
> There is yet another class of committees which monitors the functioning of certain executives. Some of these committees are the Committee on Public Accounts, Committee on Estimates, Committees on Subordinate Legislation and the Committee on Government Assurances.

Deadlocks may sometimes arise during the functioning of the Parliament. Here are the details:

> ## IN CASE OF A DEADLOCK BETWEEN THE LOK SABHA AND THE RAJYA SABHA
>
> If the Lok Sabha and Rajya Sabha disagree over Bills, other than Money Bills and Constitution Amendment Bills, the President summons a Joint Sitting of both Houses. This happens when a Bill is passed by one House and is rejected by the other House or the Houses disagree on the amendments to be made in the Bill or more than six months have elapsed from the date of receipt of the Bill by the other House without the Bill being passed by it. The Speaker of the Lok Sabha presides over Joint Sittings. So far, only three Joint Sittings have been held to resolve a deadlock on Bills between them:
> 1. On 6 and 9 May 1961 for the Dowry Prohibition Bill, 1959;
> 2. On 17 May 1978 for the Banking Service Commission (Repeal) Bill, 1977;
> 3. On 26 March 2002 for the Prevention of Terrorism Bill, 2002.

APPENDIX 1: OUTSTANDING PARLIAMENTARIANS

The 'Outstanding Parliamentarian Award' is an award bestowed upon such members of Parliament who have made invaluable contributions and set high standards in the discharge of their duties as parliamentarians. The award was instituted by the Indian Parliamentary Group in 1995 and is given each year to a sitting member of Parliament. Hereunder is a short introduction to the recipients.

CHANDRA SHEKHAR

Chandra Shekhar was born on 1 July 1927 in Ibrahimpatti, in Uttar Pradesh. He joined politics while still a student and was known for his fire-brand idealism and revolutionary fervour. After his Master's degree in Political Science from Allahabad University (1950–51), he joined the Socialist Movement. His rebellious streak earned him the title of Young Turk. He was soon elected Secretary of the District Praja Socialist Party, Ballia.

In 1962, Chandra Shekhar was elected to the Rajya Sabha from Uttar Pradesh. As member of Parliament, he raised issues related to the poor and the downtrodden. He was the President of the Janata Party from 1977 to 1988. He became the Prime Minister of India on 10 November 1990 and continued till 21 June 1991.

Chandra Shekhar was the first recipient of the Outstanding Parliamentarian Award in 1995.

SOMNATH CHATTERJEE

Somnath Chatterjee was born on 25 July 1929 in Tezpur, Assam. He had his education in Calcutta and in the United Kingdom, where he became a barrister from the Middle Temple. After his return, he became an advocate in the Calcutta High Court.

In 1971, Somnath Chatterjee was elected to the Lok Sabha in an interim election after the death of his father who represented that constituency. Since then, he was elected to the Lok Sabha a number of times and in 2004 became its member for the tenth time.

Somnath Chatterjee was unanimously elected as Speaker of the Fourteenth Lok Sabha in 2004. His impartial conduct of the proceedings of the House during the trust vote in 2008 won him widespread appreciation, but his own party disliked this and ultimately expelled him. During his tenure, Somnath Chatterjee tried to infuse greater transparency and accountability in the working of the Lok Sabha.

Somnath Chatterjee received the award for 1996.

PRANAB MUKHERJEE

Pranab Mukherjee was born in Birbhum district of West Bengal to freedom fighter parents on 11 December 1935. After completing his education, he started teaching at a college and also became a journalist.

Inspired by his father's nationalistic ideals, Pranab Mukherjee plunged into full-time public life following his election to the Upper House of Parliament in 1969. Under the guidance of the late Prime Minister Indira Gandhi he rose to great heights in Indian politics.

At different points in time, he held various important portfolios like Finance, Commerce, External Affairs, and so on. He was the Leader of the Lok Sabha from 2004 to 2012.

In 2012, he contested the presidential elections and became the President of India.

Pranab Mukherjee received the award for 1997.

S. JAIPAL REDDY

S. Jaipal Reddy was born on 16 January 1942, in Mahbubnagar district (in current-day Telangana). He studied at Osmania University, Hyderabad, and earned a post-graduate degree in English.

Reddy served as a member of the Andhra Pradesh Legislative Assembly for four terms, beginning 1969. He was elected to the Eighth, Twelfth, Thirteenth, Fourteenth and Fifteenth Lok Sabhas and was also a member of the Rajya Sabha from 1990 to 1996 and from 1997 to 1999.

After being elected in 2004, Reddy assumed charge as the Union Minister of Information & Broadcasting and Culture, and as the Urban Development Minister, a year later.

Reddy received the award for 1998.

LAL KRISHNA ADVANI

Born on 8 November 1927 in Karachi in present-day Pakistan, Lal Krishna Advani received his education in Karachi and Hyderabad.

Advani joined the Rashtriya Swayamsevak Sangh (RSS) at the early age of fourteen and shifted his base to New Delhi to assist Atal Bihari Vajpayee. He then joined the Organiser, a political journal of the Jana Sangh as an assistant editor.

In 1970, Advani was elected as the President of the Bharatiya Jana Sangh, the precursor to the Bharatiya Janata Party (BJP). He served as the Union Minister for Information and Broadcasting from 1977 to 1979 and became the President of the BJP in 1986. He was elected to the Rajya Sabha and the Lok Sabha for more than three terms. Advani was first the Home Minister and later the Deputy Prime Minister in the cabinet of Atal Bihari Vajpayee (1999–2004). In 2014, he was re-elected to the Lok Sabha from Gandhinagar, Gujarat.

Advani received the award for 1999.

ARJUN SINGH

Arjun Singh was born on 5 November 1930 in Sidhi (in current-day Madhya Pradesh). He studied at Allahabad University and Agra University and went on to earn a degree in Law.

Arjun Singh was elected a member of the Madhya Pradesh Legislative Assembly in 1957 and became the Chief Minister in 1980. He was elected to the Lok Sabha soon after and became the Union Minister for Commerce. In 1991, he was again elected to the Lok Sabha and was part of the Congress government at the Centre, at various points of time. Some of the ministries he held were Communications and Human Resource Development.

Arjun Singh received the award for the year 2000.

JASWANT SINGH

Jaswant Singh was born on 3 January 1938, in Barmer district of Rajasthan. He joined the Air Force and then shifted to the cavalry unit of the Indian Army.

Although Jaswant Singh had received offers for joining the Jana Sangh and the Swatantra Party, it was his significant meeting with Atal Bihari Vajpayee that launched his political career. He has been elected to the Lok Sabha for four terms and has served in the Rajya Sabha for five terms. He has held many portfolios including Finance and External Affairs.

Jaswant Singh received the award for 2001.

MANMOHAN SINGH

Manmohan Singh was born on 26 September 1932 in undivided India's Punjab province. He was part of the faculty at the Delhi School of Economics in the 1960s. He was the Economic Adviser to the Prime Minister in the 1970s and held the chair of the Governor of the Reserve Bank of India (RBI) from 1982 to 1985.

Manmohan Singh was elected to the Rajya Sabha in 1991. He was Leader of the Opposition in Rajya Sabha from 1998 to 2004. As the Union Finance Minister in 1991, he brought in reforms by devaluating the rupee, lowering the taxes, privatising the state-run industries and encouraging foreign investment. He took over as the Prime Minister in 2004 and continued for two full terms.

Manmohan Singh received the award for 2002.

SHARAD PAWAR

Sharad Pawar was born on 12 December 1940 in Pune. He graduated in Commerce and then became a member of the Maharashtra Legislative Assembly in 1967. He held various ministries in the Maharashtra state government in the 1970s before serving as the Chief Minister of the state for four terms.

Pawar was elected to the Eighth Lok Sabha in 1984 and the Tenth Lok Sabha in 1991. He was soon given the charge of the Union Defence portfolio. Pawar was elected to the Lok Sabha for many more terms and was in charge of various ministries like Agriculture and Consumer Affairs, Food and Public Distribution. In 2014, he became a member of the Rajya Sabha. He also served as the President of International Cricket Council from 2010 to 2012.

Pawar received the award for 2003.

SUSHMA SWARAJ

Sushma Swaraj was born on 14 February 1952 in Haryana. She graduated in Arts from Ambala, and earned a degree in Law from Punjab University.

In 1970, Swaraj began her political career with the student's wing of BJP—Akhil Bharatiya Vidyarthi Parishad (ABVP). A few years later, she became a member of the Haryana Legislative Assembly and a minister in the Haryana state government at the tender age of twenty-five. She was elected as a member of the Rajya Sabha in 1990 and held the position until she was elected to the Eleventh Lok Sabha in 1996.

In the Atal Bihari Vajpayee government of 1996 and 1998, Swaraj held the Information and Broadcasting portfolio. She resigned from the Union Cabinet to take over as the first woman Chief Minister of Delhi in October 1998. In 2006, she was elected to the Rajya Sabha and served as the Deputy Leader of the BJP there. She was elected to the Lok Sabha and went on to become the Leader of Opposition in the Fifteenth Lok Sabha. She was re-elected to the Lok Sabha in 2014 and became the Union Minister for External Affairs in the cabinet of Narendra Modi.

Swaraj received the award for 2004.

P. CHIDAMBARAM

P. Chidambaram was born in 1945 in Tamil Nadu and educated in Madras. He became a lawyer and later obtained his MBA degree from the Harvard Business School in 1968.

Chidambaram became a lawyer in the Madras High Court and joined the Congress Party. In 1984, he was elected as an MP from Sivaganga, a constituency he represented for six more terms. In 1985, Rajiv Gandhi inducted him into his cabinet and over the years, he held various portfolios. In 2004, Chidambaram became the Union Finance Minister in former Prime Minister Manmohan Singh's cabinet. In 2008, he became the Union Home Minister, before returning to the Finance Ministry a few years later.

Chidambaram received the award for 2005.

MANI SHANKAR AIYAR

Mani Shankar Aiyar was born on 10 April 1941 in Lahore (now in Pakistan). He was educated at the Doon School, St Stephen's College and Trinity Hall, Cambridge University.

Aiyar was elected to the Lok Sabha in 1991, 2004 and 2009. He was part of various committees like those on rural development, and central advisory committee for the pilot scheme called the Pradhan Mantri Adarsh Gram Yojana. Aiyar has held ministries like Panchayati Raj, Petroleum and Natural Gas, Youth Affairs and Sports, and Development of Northeastern Region. In 2010, he was nominated to the Rajya Sabha.

Aiyar received the award for 2006.

PRIYA RANJAN DASMUNSI

Priya Ranjan Dasmunsi was born on 13 November 1945 in present-day Bangladesh. He completed his education in Law from the University of Calcutta.

Dasmunsi was a devoted NCC cadet since college days and served as the President of the Calcutta University Students' Union during 1967-70. In 1970, he became the President of the Youth Congress in West Bengal and was elected to the Fifth Lok Sabha a year later.

In 1984, Dasmunsi was elected to the Eighth Lok Sabha and soon became the Union Minister of State for Commerce. He won three more terms as member of the Lok Sabha and held important positions like the Chief Whip of the Congress

Parliamentary Party, the Union Cabinet Minister for Water Resources and Minister of Information and Broadcasting. He also served as the President of the All India Football Federation.

Dasmunsi received the award for 2007.

MOHAN SINGH

Mohan Singh was born on 4 March 1945 in Deoria (in Uttar Pradesh). He earned an MA degree from the University of Allahabad. While in college, he became actively involved in student politics. Later, in 1977, Singh was elected as a member of the Uttar Pradesh Legislative Assembly and became a minister in the state government shortly thereafter. He was elected to the Tenth Lok Sabha in 1991.

In the following years, Mohan Singh was elected to the Lok Sabha and was a member of various Parliamentary Committees like the Business Advisory Committee, Committee of Privileges, House Committee and Committee on Home Affairs.

Mohan Singh received the award for 2008.

MURLI MANOHAR JOSHI

Murli Manohar Joshi was born in Nainital on 5 January 1934. He completed his MSc and doctorate from Allahabad University and joined the institution as a professor of Physics. He retired in 1994 as the Head of the Department of Physics.

At a very young age, Joshi came in touch with the Rashtriya Swayamsevak Sangh (RSS) and actively participated in their programmes. In 1977, he was elected as an MP from the Almora constituency. In 1980, when the BJP came into being, Joshi became one of its General Secretaries. In Atal Bihari Vajpayee's cabinet, he held the Home Affairs portfolio briefly before going on to become the Human Resource Development Minister. In 2014, he was elected to the Lok Sabha from the

Kanpur constituency. During his political career, he served as a member of the Rajya Sabha for many years.

Joshi received the award for 2009.

ARUN JAITLEY

Arun Jaitley was born in 1952 in New Delhi. He studied at St Xavier's School and graduated in Commerce from Shri Ram College of Commerce before earning his Law degree from the University of Delhi. He had a successful career in law and is a Senior Advocate in the Supreme Court of India.

While at university, Jaitley became a member of ABVP. When the BJP came into being in 1980, he was made the President of the youth wing of the party and before the 1999 general elections he was made the party spokesperson.

In the Vajpayee cabinet of 1999, Jaitley was appointed as the Minister of State for Information and Broadcasting (Independent Charge). Over the years, he has held various ministries like Disinvestment and Law, and Justice and Company Affairs. In 2009, he was chosen as the Leader of the Opposition in the Rajya Sabha. In 2014, when the Narendra Modi government came to power, he became a Cabinet Minister.

Jaitley received the award for 2010.

KARAN SINGH

Karan Singh was born in Cannes in France on 9 March 1931. He is son of Maharaja Hari Singh of Jammu and Kashmir. He was educated at the Doon School, Jammu and Kashmir University and Delhi University.

In his initial days, Karan Singh was the regent of the Jammu and Kashmir state and was made the Sadar-i-Riyasat in 1952. Later, he also served as its Governor. He held various important positions including those of the Chancellor of the Jammu and

Kashmir University and the Banaras Hindu University (BHU). Singh was a member of the Fourth, Fifth, Sixth and Seventh Lok Sabhas.

In 1967, Karan Singh was the Union Minister of Tourism and Civil Aviation and subsequently held ministries like Health and Family Planning, Education, Social Welfare and Culture.

Karan Singh received the award for 2011.

SHARAD YADAV

Sharad Yadav was born on 1 July 1947 in Madhya Pradesh. He completed his education earning a degree in Electrical Engineering. He was the President of the Students' Union at the Jabalpur Engineering College.

In 1974, Sharad Yadav was elected to the Fifth Lok Sabha in a bye-election. He was re-elected to the Sixth Lok Sabha and became President of the Yuva Janata Dal. He became a member of the Rajya Sabha in 1986 and held several positions in the Janata Dal party. After being elected to the Thirteenth Lok Sabha in 1999, he held various Union Cabinet Ministries like Civil Aviation, Labour and Consumer Affairs, Food and Public Distribution. In 2004, he again became a member of the Rajya Sabha and five years later was re-elected to the Lok Sabha for his Seventh term.

Sharad Yadav received the award for 2012.

APPENDIX 2: SOME FAMOUS SPEECHES ASSOCIATED WITH THE PARLIAMENT OF INDIA*

JAWAHARLAL NEHRU'S 'TRYST WITH DESTINY' SPEECH

The famous Tryst with Destiny speech was delivered on the eve of India's independence, towards midnight on 14 August 1947 at the Fifth Session of the Constituent Assembly of India in the Constitution Hall, New Delhi. The extract of the same is given below:

> Long years ago we made a tryst with destiny, and now the time comes when we shall redeem our pledge, not wholly or in full measure, but very substantially. At the stroke of the midnight hour, when the world sleeps, India will awake to life and freedom. A moment comes, which comes but rarely in history, when we step out from the old to the new, when an age ends, and when the soul of a nation, long suppressed, finds utterance. It is fitting that at this solemn moment we take the pledge of dedication to the service of India and her people and to the still larger cause of humanity.

---

*The speeches are taken from the Constituent Assembly Debates, listed on parliamentofindia.nic.in

At the dawn of history India started on her unending quest, and trackless centuries are filled with her striving and the grandeur of her successes and her failures. Through good and ill fortune alike she has never lost sight of that quest or forgotten the ideals which gave her strength. We end today a period of ill fortune and India discovers herself again. The achievement we celebrate today is but a step, an opening of opportunity, to the greater triumphs and achievements that await us. Are we brave enough and wise enough to grasp this opportunity and accept the challenge of the future?

Freedom and power bring responsibility. That responsibility rests upon this Assembly, a sovereign body representing the sovereign people of India. Before the birth of freedom we have endured all the pains of labour and our hearts are heavy with the memory of this sorrow. Some of those pains continue even now. Nevertheless the past is over and it is the future that beckons to us now.

That future is not one of ease or resting but of incessant striving so that we might fulfil the pledges we have so often taken and the one we shall take today. The service of India means the service of the millions who suffer. It means the ending of poverty and ignorance and disease and inequality of opportunity. The ambition of the greatest man of our generation has been to wipe every tear from every eye. That may be beyond us but as long as there are tears and suffering, so long our work will not be over.

And so we have to labour and to work and work hard to give reality to our dreams. Those dreams are for India, but they are also for the world, for all the nations and peoples are too closely knit together today for any one of them to imagine that it can live apart.

Peace has been said to be indivisible, so is freedom, so is prosperity now, and so also is disaster in this One World that can no longer be split into isolated fragments. To the people of India, whose representatives we are, we make appeal to join us with faith and confidence in this great adventure. This is no time for petty and destructive criticism, no time for ill-will or blaming others. We have to build the noble mansion of free India where all her children may dwell.

SARVEPALLI RADHAKRISHNAN'S 'THE DAWN OF FREEDOM' SPEECH

The Dawn of Freedom speech was delivered on the eve of India's independence on 14 August 1947 at the Fifth Session of the Constituent Assembly of India in the Constitution Hall, New Delhi. The extract of the same is below:

> History and legend will grow round this day. It marks a milestone in the march of our democracy. A significant date it is in the drama of the Indian people who are trying to rebuild and transform themselves. Through a long night of waiting, a night full of fateful portents and silent prayers for the dawn of freedom, of haunting spectres of hunger and death, our sentinels kept watch, the lights were burning bright till at last the dawn is breaking and we greet it with the utmost enthusiasm. When we are passing from a state of serfdom, a state of slavery and subjection to one of freedom and liberation, it is an occasion for rejoicing. That it is being effected in such an orderly and dignified way is a matter for gratification.

Mr Attlee spoke with visible pride in the House of Commons when he said that this is the first great instance of a strong Imperialist power transferring its authority to a subject people whom it ruled with force and firmness for nearly two centuries. For a parallel he cited the British withdrawal from South Africa; but it is nothing comparable in scale and circumstances to the British withdrawal from this country. When we see what the Dutch are doing in Indonesia, when we see how the French are clinging to their possessions, we cannot but admire the political sagacity and courage of the British people.

We on our side, have also added a chapter to the history of the World. Look at the way in which subject peoples in history won their freedom. Let us also consider the methods by which power was acquired. How, did men like Washington, Napoleon, Cromwell, Lenin, Hitler and Mussolini get into power? Look at the methods of blood and steel, of terrorism and assassination, of bloodshed and anarchy by which these so-called great men of the world came into the possession of power. Here in this land under the leadership of one who will go down in history, as perhaps the greatest man of our age, we have opposed patience to fury, quietness of spirit to bureaucratic tyranny and are acquiring power through peaceful and civilised methods. What is the result? The transition is being effected with the least bitterness, with utterly no kind of hatred at all. The very fact that we are appointing Lord Mountbatten as the Governor General of India, shows the spirit of understanding and friendliness in which this whole transition is being effected.

B. R. AMBEDKAR'S 'GRAMMAR OF ANARCHY' SPEECH

The Grammar of Anarchy speech was delivered on 25 November 1949 at the Constituent Assembly of India in the Constitution Hall, New Delhi. Read the excerpt below.

> If we wish to maintain democracy not merely in form, but also in fact, what must we do? The first thing in my judgement we must do is to hold fast to constitutional methods of achieving our social and economic objectives. It means we must abandon the bloody methods of revolution. It means that we must abandon the method of civil disobedience, non-cooperation and satyagraha. When there was no way left for constitutional methods for achieving economic and social objectives, there was a great deal of justification for unconstitutional methods. But where constitutional methods are open, there can be no justification for these unconstitutional methods. These methods are nothing but the Grammar of Anarchy and the sooner they are abandoned, the better for us.

APPENDIX 3: TABLE OF PRECEDENCE

In India, the Table of Precedence is an official list of functionaries and office bearers in a descending order of importance, according to their rank and office. It is the order in which they are to be acknowledged and seated.

The list includes:

1. President
2. Vice President
3. Prime Minister
4. Governors of states within their respective states
5. Former Presidents
5A. Deputy Prime Minister
6. Chief Justice of India, Speaker of Lok Sabha
7. Cabinet Ministers of the Union, Chief Ministers of states within their respective states, Deputy Chairman of Planning Commission, Former Prime Ministers, Leaders of Opposition in Rajya Sabha and Lok Sabha
7A. Holders of Bharat Ratna decoration
8. Ambassadors Extraordinary and Plenipotentiary and High Commissioners of Commonwealth countries accredited to India, Chief Ministers of states outside their respective states, Governors of states outside their respective states
9. Judges of Supreme Court
9A. Chairperson of Union Public Service Commission, Chief

Election Commissioner, Comptroller & Auditor General of India

10. Deputy Chairman of Rajya Sabha, Deputy Chief Ministers of states, Deputy Speaker of Lok Sabha, Members of the Planning Commission, Ministers of State of the Union (and any other Minister in the Ministry of Defence for defence matters)
11. Attorney General of India, Cabinet Secretary, Lieutenant Governors within their respective union territories
12. Chiefs of Staff holding the rank of full General or equivalent rank
13. Envoys Extraordinary and Ministers Plenipotentiary accredited to India
14. Chairmen and Speakers of State Legislatures within their respective states, Chief Justices of High Courts within their respective jurisdictions
15. Cabinet Ministers in states within their respective states, Chief Ministers of union territories and Chief Executive Councillor, Delhi within their respective union territories, Deputy Ministers of the Union
16. Officiating Chiefs of Staff holding the rank of Lieutenant General or equivalent rank
17. Chairman of Central Administrative Tribunal, Chairman of Minorities Commission, Chairperson of National Commission for Scheduled Castes, Chairperson of National Commission for Scheduled Tribes, Chief Justices of High Courts outside their respective jurisdictions, present judges of High Courts within their respective jurisdictions
18. Cabinet Ministers in states outside their respective states, Chairmen and Speakers of State Legislatures outside their respective states, Chairman of Monopolies and Restrictive Trade Practices Commission, Deputy

Chairmen and Deputy Speakers of State Legislatures within their respective states, Ministers of State in states within their respective states, Ministers of union territories and Executive Councillors of Delhi within their respective union territories, Speakers of Legislative Assemblies in union territories and Chairman of Delhi Metropolitan Council within their respective union territories

19. Chief Commissioners of union territories not having Councils of Ministers (within their respective union territories), Deputy Ministers in states within their respective states, Deputy Speakers of Legislative Assemblies in union territories and Deputy Chairman of the Metropolitan Council Delhi (within their respective union territories)
20. Deputy Chairmen and Deputy Speakers of State Legislatures outside their respective states, Ministers of state in states outside their respective states, present judges of High Courts outside their respective jurisdictions
21. Members of Parliament
22. Deputy Ministers in state outside their respective states
23. Army Commanders/ Vice Chief of the Army Staff or equivalent in other services, Chief Secretaries to state governments within their respective states, Commissioner for Linguistic Minorities, Commissioner for Scheduled Castes and Scheduled Tribes, Members of Minorities Commission, Members of National Commission for Scheduled Castes, Members of National Commission for Scheduled Tribes, Officers of the rank of full General or equivalent rank, Secretaries to the Government of India (including officers holding this office ex-officio), Secretary of Minorities Commission, Secretary of Scheduled Castes and Scheduled Tribes Commission, Secretary to the President, Secretary to the Prime Minister, Secretary of

Rajya Sabha/Lok Sabha, Solicitor General, Vice Chairman of Central Administrative Tribunal

24. Officers of the rank of Lieutenant General or equivalent rank

25. Additional Secretaries to the Government of India, Additional Solicitor General, Advocate Generals of States, Chairman of Tariff Commission, Chargé d'affaires and Acting High Commissioners en pied and ad interim, Chief Ministers of union territories and Chief Executive Councillor of Delhi (outside their respective union territories), Chief Secretaries of state governments outside their respective states, Deputy Comptroller and Auditor General, Deputy Speakers of Legislative Assemblies in union territories and Deputy Chairman of Delhi Metropolitan Council (outside their respective union territories), Director of Central Bureau of Investigation, Director General of Border Security Force, Director General of Central Reserve Police Force, Director of Intelligence Bureau, Lieutenant Governors outside their respective union territories, Members of Central Administrative Tribunal, Members of Monopolies and Restrictive Trade Practices Commission, Members of Union Public Service Commission, Ministers of union territories and Executive Councillors of Delhi (outside their respective union territories), Principal Staff Officers of the Armed Forces of the rank of major General or equivalent rank, Speakers of Legislative Assemblies in union territories and Chairman of Delhi Metropolitan Council (outside their respective union territories)

26. Joint Secretaries to the Government of India and officers of equivalent rank, officers of the rank of Major-General or equivalent rank

APPENDIX 4: ELECTION SYMBOLS (AS OF 2014)

SYMBOLS RESERVED FOR INDIAN NATIONAL POLITICAL PARTIES

Elephant
Bahujan Samaj Party
(In all states/UTs except in the state of Assam, where its candidates will have to choose a symbol from out of the list of free symbols specified by the Commission)

LOTUS
Bharatiya Janata Party

EARS OF CORN & SICKLE
Communist Party of India

HAMMER, SICKLE & STAR
Communist Party of India (Marxist)

HAND
Indian National Congress

CLOCK
Nationalist Congress Party

SOME STATE PARTIES AND THEIR ELECTION SYMBOLS

1. Andhra Pradesh	1. Telangana Rashtra Samithi	 Car

	2. Telugu Desam	**Bicycle**
2. Arunachal Pradesh	1. All India Trinamool Congress	**Flowers & Grass**
	2. People's Party of Arunachal	**Maize**
3. Assam	1. All India United Democratic Front	**Lock & Key**
	2. Asom Gana Parishad	**Elephant**

Contd.

	3. Bodoland People's Front	**Nangal**
4. Bihar	1. Janata Dal (United)	**Arrow**
	2. Lok Jan Shakti Party	**Bungalow**
	3. Rashtriya Janata Dal	**Hurricane Lamp**
5. Goa	1. Maharashtrawadi Gomantak	**Lion**

6. Haryana	1. Haryana Janhit Congress (BL)	Tractor
	2. Indian National Lok Dal	Spectacles
7. Jammu and Kashmir	1. Jammu and Kashmir National Conference	Plough
	2. Jammu and Kashmir National Panthers Party	Bicycle
	3. Jammu and Kashmir Peoples Democratic Party	Ink Pot & Pen

Contd.

8. Jharkhand	1. AJSU Party	Banana
	2. Jharkhand Mukti Morcha	Bow & Arrow
	3. Jharkhand Vikas Morcha (Prajatantrik)	Comb
	4. Rashtriya Janata Dal	Hurricane Lamp
9. Karnataka	1. Janata Dal (Secular)	A Lady Farmer Carrying Paddy on Her Head

	2. Karnataka Janatha Paksha	Coconut
10. Kerala	1. Janata Dal (Secular)	A Lady Farmer Carrying Paddy on Her Head
	2. Kerala Congress (M)	Two Leaves
	3. Indian Union Muslim League	Ladder
11. Maharashtra	1. Maharashtra Navnirman Sena	Railway Engine

Contd.

	2. Shiv Sena	Bow & Arrow
12. Manipur	1. All India Trinamool Congress	Flowers & Grass
	2. Manipur State Congress Party	Cultivator Cutting Crop
	3. Naga People's Front	Cock
	4. People's Democratic Alliance	Crown

13. Meghalaya	1. United Democratic Party	Drum
	2. Hill State People's Democratic Party	Lion
	3. National People's Party	Book
14. Mizoram	1. Mizo National Front	Star

Contd.

	2. Mizoram People's Conference	Electric Bulb
	3. Zoram Nationalist Party	Sun (Without Rays)
15. Nagaland	1. Naga People's Front	Cock
16. National Capital Territory of Delhi	1. Aam Aadmi Party	Broom
17. Odisha	1. Biju Janata Dal	Conch

18. Puducherry	1. All India Anna Dravida Munnetra Kazhagam	Two Leaves
	2. All India N.R. Congress	Jug
	3. Dravida Munnetra Kazhagam	Rising Sun
	4. Pattali Makkal Katchi	Mango

Contd.

19. Punjab	1. Shiromani Akali Dal	**Scales**
20. Sikkim	1. Sikkim Democratic Front	**Umbrella**
21. Tamil Nadu	1. All India Anna Dravida Munnetra Kazhagam	**Two Leaves**
	2. Dravida Munnetra Kazhagam	**Rising Sun**
	3. Desiya Murpokku Dravida Kazhagam	**Nagara**

22. Uttar Pradesh	1. Rashtriya Lok Dal	**Hand Pump**
	2. Samajwadi Party	**Bicycle**
23. West Bengal	1. All India Forward Bloc	**Lion**
	2. All India Trinamool Congress	**Flowers & Grass**
	3. Revolutionary Socialist Party	**Spade & Stoker**

APPENDIX 5: UNION, STATE AND CONCURRENT LISTS

LIST I—UNION LIST
1. Defence of India and every part thereof including preparation for defence and all such acts as may be conducive in times of war to its prosecution and after its termination to effective demobilisation.
2. Naval, military and air forces; any other armed forces of the Union.
2A. Deployment of any armed force of the Union or any other force subject to the control of the Union or any contingent or unit thereof in any state in aid of the civil power; powers, jurisdiction, privileges and liabilities of the members of such forces while on such deployment.
3. Delimitation of cantonment areas, local self-government in such areas, the constitution and powers within such areas of cantonment authorities and the regulation of house accommodation (including the control of rents) in such areas.
4. Naval, military and air force works.
5. Arms, firearms, ammunition and explosives.
6. Atomic energy and mineral resources necessary for its production.
7. Industries declared by Parliament by law to be necessary for the purpose of defence or for the prosecution of war.

8. Central Bureau of Intelligence and Investigation (CBI).
9. Preventive detention for reasons connected with Defence, Foreign Affairs, or the security of India; persons subjected to such detention.
10. Foreign affairs; all matters which bring the Union into relation with any foreign country.
11. Diplomatic, consular and trade representation.
12. United Nations Organisation.
13. Participation in international conferences, associations and other bodies and implementing of decisions made thereat.
14. Entering into treaties and agreements with foreign countries and implementing of treaties, agreements and conventions with foreign countries.
15. War and peace.
16. Foreign jurisdiction.
17. Citizenship, naturalisation and aliens.
18. Extradition.
19. Admission into, and emigration and expulsion from, India; passports and visas.
20. Pilgrimages to places outside India.
21. Piracies and crimes committed on the high seas or in the air; offences against the law of nations committed on land or the high seas or in the air.
22. Railways.
23. Highways declared by or under law made by Parliament to be national highways.
24. Shipping and navigation on inland waterways, declared by Parliament by law to be national waterways, as regards mechanically propelled vessels; the rule of the road on such waterways.
25. Maritime shipping and navigation, including shipping and navigation on tidal waters; provision of education

and training for the mercantile marine and regulation of such education and training provided by states and other agencies.
26. Lighthouses, including lightships, beacons and other provision for the safety of shipping and aircraft.
27. Ports declared by or under law made by Parliament or existing law to be major ports, including their delimitation, and the constitution and powers of port authorities therein.
28. Port quarantine, including hospitals connected therewith; seamen's and marine hospitals.
29. Airways; aircraft and air navigation; provision of aerodromes; regulation and organisation of air traffic and of aerodromes; provision for aeronautical education and training and regulation of such education and training provided by states and other agencies.
30. Carriage of passengers and goods by railway, sea or air, or by national waterways in mechanically propelled vessels.
31. Posts and telegraphs; telephones, wireless, broadcasting and other like forms of communication.
32. Property of the Union and the revenue therefrom, but as regards property situated in a state subject to legislation by the state, save in so far as Parliament by law otherwise provides.
33 Omitted.
34. Courts of wards for the estates of rulers of Indian states.
35. Public debt of the Union.
36. Currency, coinage and legal tender; foreign exchange.
37. Foreign loans.
38. Reserve Bank of India.
39. Post Office Savings Bank.
40. Lotteries organised by the Government of India or the government of a state.

41. Trade and commerce with foreign countries; import and export across customs frontiers; definition of customs frontiers.
42. Inter-state trade and commerce.
43. Incorporation, regulation and winding up of trading corporations, including banking, insurance and financial corporations, but not including co-operative societies.
44. Incorporation, regulation and winding up of corporations, whether trading or not, with objects not confined to one state, but not including universities.
45. Banking.
46. Bills of exchange, cheques, promissory notes and other like instruments.
47. Insurance.
48. Stock exchanges and futures markets.
49. Patents, inventions and designs; copyright; trade-marks and merchandise marks.
50. Establishment of standards of weight and measure.
51. Establishment of standards of quality for goods to be exported out of India or transported from one state to another.
52. Industries, the control of which by the Union is declared by Parliament by law to be expedient in the public interest.
53. Regulation and development of oilfields and mineral oil resources; petroleum and petroleum products; other liquids and substances declared by Parliament by law to be dangerously inflammable.
54. Regulation of mines and mineral development to the extent to which such regulation and development under the control of the Union is declared by Parliament by law to be expedient in the public interest.
55. Regulation of labour and safety in mines and oilfields.

56. Regulation and development of inter-state rivers and river valleys to the extent to which such regulation and development under the control of the Union is declared by Parliament by law to be expedient in the public interest.
57. Fishing and fisheries beyond territorial waters.
58. Manufacture, supply and distribution of salt by Union agencies; regulation and control of manufacture, supply and distribution of salt by other agencies.
59. Cultivation, manufacture, and sale for export, of opium.
60. Sanctioning of cinematograph films for exhibition.
61. Industrial disputes concerning union employees.
62. The institutions known at the commencement of this Constitution as the National Library, the Indian Museum, the Imperial War Museum, the Victoria Memorial and the Indian War Memorial, and any other like institution financed by the Government of India wholly or in part and declared by Parliament by law to be an institution of national importance.
63. The institutions known at the commencement of this Constitution as the Benares Hindu University, the Aligarh Muslim University and the Delhi University; the University established in pursuance of article 371E; any other institution declared by Parliament by law to be an institution of national importance.
64. Institutions for scientific or technical education financed by the Government of India wholly or in part and declared by Parliament by law to be institutions of national importance.
65. Union agencies and institutions for—
    1. professional, vocational or technical training, including the training of police officers; or
    2. the promotion of special studies or research; or
    3. scientific or technical assistance in the investigation

or detection of crime.
66. Co-ordination and determination of standards in institutions for higher education or research and scientific and technical institutions.
67. Ancient and historical monuments and records, and archaeological sites and remains, declared by or under law made by Parliament to be of national importance.
68. The Survey of India, the Geological, Botanical, Zoological and Anthropological Surveys of India; meteorological organisations.
69. Census.
70. Union Public Service; All-India Services; Union Public Service Commission.
71. Union pensions, that is to say, pensions payable by the Government of India or out of the Consolidated Fund of India.
72. Elections to Parliament, to the legislatures of states and to the offices of President and Vice President; the Election Commission.
73. Salaries and allowances of members of Parliament, the Chairman and Deputy Chairman of the Council of States and the Speaker and Deputy Speaker of the House of the People.
74. Powers, privileges and immunities of each House of Parliament and of the members and the Committees of each House; enforcement of attendance of persons for giving evidence or producing documents before committees of Parliament or commissions appointed by Parliament.
75. Emoluments, allowances, privileges, and rights in respect of leave of absence, of the President and Governors; salaries and allowances of the Ministers for the Union; the salaries, allowances, and rights in respect of leave of

absence and other conditions of service of the Comptroller and Auditor General.

76. Audit of the accounts of the Union and of the states.
77. Constitution, organisation, jurisdiction and powers of the Supreme Court (including contempt of such Court), and the fees taken therein; persons entitled to practise before the Supreme Court.
78. Constitution and organisation (including vacations) of the High Courts except provisions as to officers and servants of High Courts; persons entitled to practise before the High Courts.
79. Extension of the jurisdiction of a High Court to, and exclusion of the jurisdiction of a High Court from, any union territory.
80. Extension of the powers and jurisdiction of members of a police force belonging to any state to any area outside that state, but not so as to enable the police of one state to exercise powers and jurisdiction in any area outside that state without the consent of the government of the state in which such area is situated; extension of the powers and jurisdiction of members of a police force belonging to any state to railway areas outside that state.
81. Inter-state migration; inter-state quarantine.
82. Taxes on income other than agricultural income.
83. Duties of customs including export duties.
84. Duties of excise on tobacco and other goods manufactured or produced in India except—
    1. alcoholic liquors for human consumption;
    2. opium, Indian hemp and other narcotic drugs and narcotics, but including medicinal and toilet preparations containing alcohol or any substance included in sub-paragraph (b) of this entry.

85. Corporation tax.
86. Taxes on the capital value of the assets, exclusive of agricultural land, of individuals and companies; taxes on the capital of companies.
87. Estate duty in respect of property other than agricultural land.
88. Duties in respect of succession to property other than agricultural land.
89. Terminal taxes on goods or passengers, carried by railway, sea or air; taxes on railway fares and freights.
90. Taxes other than stamp duties on transactions in stock exchanges and futures markets.
91. Rates of stamp duty in respect of bills of exchange, cheques, promissory notes, bills of lading, letters of credit, policies of insurance, transfer of shares, debentures, proxies and receipts.
92. Taxes on the sale or purchase of newspapers and on advertisements published therein.
92A. Taxes on the sale or purchase of goods other than newspapers, where such sale or purchase takes place in the course of inter-state trade or commerce.
92B. Taxes on the consignments of goods (whether the consignment is to the person making it or to any other person), where such consignment takes place in the course of inter-state trade or commerce.
93. Offences against laws with respect to any of the matters in this list.
94. Inquiries, surveys and statistics for the purpose of any of the matters in this list.
95. Jurisdiction and powers of all courts, except the Supreme Court, with respect to any of the matters in this list; admiralty jurisdiction.

96. Fees in respect of any of the matters in this list, but not including fees taken in any court.
97. Any other matter not enumerated in List II or List III including any tax not mentioned in either of those lists.

LIST II—STATE LIST

1. Public order (but not including the use of any naval, military or air force or any other armed force of the Union or of any other force subject to the control of the Union or of any contingent or unit thereof in aid of the civil power).
2. Police (including railway and village police) subject to the provisions of entry 2A of List I.
3. Officers and servants of the High Court; procedure in rent and revenue courts; fees taken in all courts except the Supreme Court.
4. Prisons, reformatories, Borstal institutions and other institutions of a like nature, and persons detained therein; arrangements with other states for the use of prisons and other institutions.
5. Local government, that is to say, the Constitution and powers of municipal corporations, improvement trusts, districts boards, mining settlement authorities and other local authorities for the purpose of local self-government or village administration.
6. Public health and sanitation; hospitals and dispensaries.
7. Pilgrimages, other than pilgrimages to places outside India.
8. Intoxicating liquors, that is to say, the production, manufacture, possession, transport, purchase and sale of intoxicating liquors.
9. Relief of the disabled and unemployable.
10. Burials and burial grounds; cremations and cremation grounds.

11. Omitted.
12. Libraries, museums and other similar institutions controlled or financed by the state; ancient and historical monuments and records other than those declared by or under law made by Parliament to be of national importance.
13. Communications, that is to say, roads, bridges, ferries, and other means of communication not specified in List I; municipal tramways; ropeways; inland waterways and traffic thereon subject to the provisions of List I and List III with regard to such waterways; vehicles other than mechanically propelled vehicles.
14. Agriculture, including agricultural education and research, protection against pests and prevention of plant diseases.
15. Preservation, protection and improvement of stock and prevention of animal diseases; veterinary training and practice.
16. Pounds and the prevention of cattle trespass.
17. Water, that is to say, water supplies, irrigation and canals, drainage and embankments, water storage and water power subject to the provisions of entry 56 of List I.
18. Land, that is to say, rights in or over land, land tenures including the relation of landlord and tenant, and the collection of rents; transfer and alienation of agricultural land; land improvement and agricultural loans; colonisation.
19. Omitted.
20. Omitted.
21. Fisheries.
22. Courts of wards subject to the provisions of entry 34 of List I; encumbered and attached estates.
23. Regulation of mines and mineral development subject to the provisions of List I with respect to regulation and

development under the control of the Union.
24. Industries subject to the provisions of entries 7 and 52 of List I.
25. Gas and gas-works.
26. Trade and commerce within the state subject to the provisions of entry 33 of List III.
27. Production, supply and distribution of goods subject to the provisions of entry 33 of List III.
28. Markets and fairs.
29. Omitted.
30. Money-lending and money-lenders; relief of agricultural indebtedness.
31. Inns and inn-keepers.
32. Incorporation, regulation and winding up of corporations, other than those specified in List I, and universities; unincorporated trading, literary, scientific, religious and other societies and associations; co-operative societies.
33. Theatres and dramatic performances; cinemas subject to the provisions of entry 60 of List I; sports, entertainments and amusements.
34. Betting and gambling.
35. Works, lands and buildings vested in or in the possession of the state.
36. Omitted.
37. Elections to the Legislature of the state subject to the provisions of any law made by Parliament.
38. Salaries and allowances of members of the Legislature of the State, of the Speaker and Deputy Speaker of the Legislative Assembly and, if there is a Legislative Council, of the Chairman and Deputy Chairman thereof.
39. Powers, privileges and immunities of the Legislative Assembly and of the members and the committees thereof,

and, if there is a Legislative Council, of that Council and of the members and the committees thereof; enforcement of attendance of persons for giving evidence or producing documents before committees of the Legislature of the State.

40. Salaries and allowances of Ministers for the State.
41. State public services; State Public Service Commission.
42. State pensions, that is to say, pensions payable by the state or out of the Consolidated Fund of the state.
43. Public debt of the state.
44. Treasure trove.
45. Land revenue, including the assessment and collection of revenue, the maintenance of land records, survey for revenue purposes and records of rights, and alienation of revenues.
46. Taxes on agricultural income.
47. Duties in respect of succession to agricultural land.
48. Estate duty in respect of agricultural land.
49. Taxes on lands and buildings.
50. Taxes on mineral rights subject to any limitations imposed by Parliament by law relating to mineral development.
51. Duties of excise on the following goods manufactured or produced in the state and countervailing duties at the same or lower rates on similar goods manufactured or produced elsewhere in India:
    1. alcoholic liquors for human consumption;
    2. opium, Indian hemp and other narcotic drugs and narcotics, but not including medicinal and toilet preparations containing alcohol or any substance included in sub-paragraph (b) of this entry.
52. Taxes on the entry of goods into a local area for consumption, use or sale therein.

53. Taxes on the consumption or sale of electricity.
54. Taxes on the sale or purchase of goods other than newspapers, subject to the provisions of entry 92A of List I.
55. Taxes on advertisements other than advertisements published in the newspapers and advertisements broadcast by radio or television.
56. Taxes on goods and passengers carried by road or on inland waterways.
57. Taxes on vehicles, whether mechanically propelled or not, suitable for use on roads, including tramcars subject to the provisions of entry 35 of List III.
58. Taxes on animals and boats.
59. Tolls.
60. Taxes on professions, trades, callings and employments.
61. Capitation taxes.
62. Taxes on luxuries, including taxes on entertainments, amusements, betting and gambling.
63. Rates of stamp duty in respect of documents other than those specified in the provisions of List I with regard to rates of stamp duty.
64. Offences against laws with respect to any of the matters in this List.
65. Jurisdiction and powers of all courts, except the Supreme Court, with respect to any of the matters in this List.
66. Fees in respect of any of the matters in this List, but not including fees taken in any court.

LIST III—CONCURRENT LIST

1. Criminal law, including all matters included in the Indian Penal Code at the commencement of this Constitution but excluding offences against laws with respect to any of the matters specified in List I or List II and excluding the use

of naval, military or air forces or any other armed forces of the Union in aid of the civil power.
2. Criminal procedure, including all matters included in the Code of Criminal Procedure at the commencement of this Constitution.
3. Preventive detention for reasons connected with the security of a state, the maintenance of public order, or the maintenance of supplies and services essential to the community; persons subjected to such detention.
4. Removal from one state to another state of prisoners, accused persons and persons subjected to preventive detention for reasons specified in entry 3 of this List.
5. Marriage and divorce; infants and minors; adoption; wills, intestacy and succession; joint family and partition; all matters in respect of which parties in judicial proceedings were immediately before the commencement of this Constitution subject to their personal law.
6. Transfer of property other than agricultural land; registration of deeds and documents.
7. Contracts, including partnership, agency, contracts of carriage, and other special forms of contracts, but not including contracts relating to agricultural land.
8. Actionable wrongs.
9. Bankruptcy and insolvency.
10. Trust and trustees.
11. Administrators-general and official trustees.
11A. Administration of Justice; constitution and organisation of all courts except the Supreme Court and the High Courts.
12. Evidence and oaths; recognition of laws, public acts and records, and judicial proceedings.
13. Civil procedure, including all matters included in the Code of Civil Procedure at the commencement of this

Constitution, limitation and arbitration.
14. Contempt of court, but not including contempt of the Supreme Court.
15. Vagrancy; nomadic and migratory tribes.
16. Lunacy and mental deficiency, including places for the reception or treatment of lunatics and mental deficients.
17. Prevention of cruelty to animals.
17A. Forests.
17B. Protection of wild animals and birds.
18. Adulteration of foodstuffs and other goods.
19. Drugs and poisons, subject to the provisions of entry 59 of List I with respect to opium.
20. Economic and social planning.
20A. Population control and family planning.
21. Commercial and industrial monopolies, combines and trust
22. Trade unions; industrial and labour disputes.
23. Social security and social insurance; employment and unemployment.
24. Welfare of labour including conditions of work, provident funds, employers' liability, workmen's compensation, invalidity and old age pensions and maternity benefits.
25. Education, including technical education, medical education and universities, subject to the provisions of entries 63, 64, 65 and 66 of List I; vocational and technical training of labour.
26. Legal, medical and other professions.
27. Relief and rehabilitation of persons displaced from their original place of residence by reason of the setting up of the Dominions of India and Pakistan.
28. Charities and charitable institutions, charitable and religious endowments and religious institutions.
29. Prevention of the extension from one state to another of

infectious or contagious diseases or pests affecting men, animals or plants.
30. Vital statistics including registration of births and deaths.
31. Ports other than those declared by or under law made by Parliament or existing law to be major ports.
32. Shipping and navigation on inland waterways as regards mechanically propelled vessels, and the rule of the road on such waterways, and the carriage of passengers and goods on inland waterways subject to the provisions of List I with respect to national waterways.
33. Trade and commerce in, and the production, supply and distribution of
    1. the products of any industry where the control of such industry by the Union is declared by Parliament by law to be expedient in the public interest, and imported goods of the same kind as such products;
    2. foodstuffs, including edible oilseeds and oils;
    3. cattle fodder, including oil cakes and other concentrates;
    4. raw cotton, whether ginned or unginned, and cotton seed; and
    5. raw jute.
33A. Weights and measures except establishment of standards.
34. Price control.
35. Mechanically propelled vehicles including the principles on which taxes on such vehicles are to be levied.
36. Factories
37. Boilers.
38. Electricity.
39. Newspapers, books and printing presses.
40. Archaeological sites and remains other than those declared by or under law made by Parliament to be of national importance.

41. Custody, management and disposal of property (including agricultural land) declared by law to be evacuee property.
42. Acquisition and requisitioning of property.
43. Recovery in a state of claims in respect of taxes and other public demands, including arrears of land-revenue and sums recoverable as such arrears, arising outside that state.
44. Stamp duties other than duties or fees collected by means of judicial stamps, but not including rates of stamp duty.
45. Inquiries and statistics for the purposes of any of the matters specified in List II or List III.
46. Jurisdiction and powers of all courts, except the Supreme Court, with respect to any of the matters in this List.
47. Fees in respect of any of the matters in this List, but not including fees taken in any court.

BIBLIOGRAPHY

Basu, Durga Das. *Introduction to the Constitution of India.* Lexis Nexis, Gurgaon: 2013.
Chandra, Bipin, Mridula Mukherjee and Aditya Mukherjee. *India Since Independence.* Penguin, New Delhi: 2008.
Guha, Ramachandra. *India After Gandhi: The History of the World's Largest Democracy.* Harper Perennial, Noida: 2008.
Johari, J.C. *The Constitution of India: A Politico-Legal Study.* Sterling Publishers, New Delhi: 2007.
Majumdar, R.C., H. C. Raychaudhuri and Kalikinkar Datta. *An Advanced History of India.* Macmillan India, New Delhi: 2001.
Sen, S. P. ed. *Dictionary of National Biography.* The Institute of Historical Studies, Calcutta: 1974.
Seth, Leila. *We, the Children of India: The Preamble to Our Constitution.* Puffin Books, New Delhi: 2010.
The Constitution of India
Encyclopedia Britannica
Guinness Book of World Records
Biographies from the Lok Sabha Secretariat

WEBSITES
http://lawmin.nic.in/olwing/coi/coi-english/coi-indexenglish.htm
http://india.gov.in/
http://indiacode.nic.in/coiweb/coifiles/amendment.htm

http://presidentofindia.nic.in/
http://vicepresidentofindia.nic.in/
http://pmindia.gov.in/en/
http://parliamentofindia.nic.in/
http://loksabha.nic.in/
http://rajyasabha.nic.in/
http://www.supremecourtofindia.nic.in/
http://eci.nic.in/
http://parliamentofindia.nic.in/ls/debates/facts.htm
http://parliamentofindia.nic.in/ls/debates/debates.htm
http://www.upsc.gov.in/
http://pib.nic.in/
http://www.rrtd.nic.in/
http://lawmin.nic.in/
http://www.rajbhasha.nic.in/
http://mha.nic.in/awards_medals
http://www.vigyanprasar.gov.in/
http://www.egazette.nic.in/
https://www.cia.gov/library/publications/the-world-factbook/